CANNABIS
SATIVA

The Essential Guide to the World's Finest Marijuana Strains

Edited by S. T. Oner
With an introduction
by Mel Thomas

Volume

2

GREEN CANDY PRESS

Cannabis Sativa:

The Essential Guide to the World's Finest Marijuana Strains, Volume 2

Published by Green Candy Press

San Francisco, CA

Copyright © 2013 Green Candy Press

ISBN 978-1-937866-03-7

Photographs © 420Clones.com, ACE Seeds, Advanced Seeds, AlphaKronik Genes, Alpine Seeds, ASG Seeds, BillBerry Farms, Blim Burn Seeds, Breedbay.co.uk, Breeder C, Buddha Seeds, Budwiser Seeds, Cali Gold Genetics, CannaBioGen, Centennial Seeds, Ch9 Female Seeds, Chillo.dk, Craig, Dane Strains, David Strange, De Sjamaan, Delicious Seeds, Delta 9 Labs, Devil's Harvest Seed Company, Dinafem Seeds, DJ Short, Don't Panic Organix, Dr. Canem and Company, Dr. Greenthumb Seeds, Dready Seeds, Dutch Flowers, Dutch Passion, Dynasty Seeds, Ed Borg, Eddie Funxta, Emerald Triangle Seeds, Eva Female Seeds, Evil Seeds, Flying Dutchmen, Gage Green Genetics, Gage Green Genetics, GBI, Gean Pool, Gibridov.net, Giorgio Alvarezzo, Green Haven Genetics, Green House Seed Co., Greenlife Seeds, Greenman420, Gro Bedre Magazine, Hemp Passion, Hex Strains, Holy Smoke Seeds, Homegrown Fantaseeds, HortiLab Seed Company, Howard Marks, Illuminati Seeds, Inkognyto, IrieVibe Seeds, JB Genetics, Jeffman, Jin Albrecht, Kaliman Seeds, Kannabia Seeds, Karma Genetics, Kingdom Organic Seeds by The Rev, Kiwiseeds, Krane Future, Lowlife Seeds, M.G.M. Genetics, Magus Genetics, Mandala Seeds, Master Thai Organic Gardens, Ministry of Cannabis, MMB&J, MoD, Mosca Seeds, Mr. Nice Seedbank, Next Generation Seed Company, No Mercy Supply, North of Seeds, Ocanabis, OG Genetics, Orgnkid, Paradise Seeds, Pistils, Pitt Bully Seeds, Positronics Seeds, Professor P, Reggae Seeds, Resin Seeds, Ringo, Riot Seeds, Rokerij Seeds, Royal Queen Seeds, Sadhu Seeds, Sagarmatha Seeds, Samsara Seeds, Sannie's Seeds, Secret Slovenian Grower, Seeds of Life, Sensi Seeds, Serious Seeds, Shantibaba, Short Stuff Seedbank, SinsemillaWorks!, Snowcap, SnowHigh Seeds, SoHum Seeds, Soma Seeds, Sonic Seeds, Spliff Seeds, Stayhigh, Stitch, Stoney Girl Gardens, Subcool and Team Green Avengers, Sweet Seeds, TH Seeds, The Blazing Pistileros, The Bulldog Seeds, The Joint Doctor, The Rev, TreeTown Seeds, Trichome Jungle Seeds, Trip Seeds, Tropical Seeds Company, Ultimate Seeds, Underground Originals, Unknown East Coast Grower, Vulkania Seeds, Weed.co.za, Whish Seeds, World of Seeds.

Cover photo: Tiger Stripe is courtesy and Copyright © Jin Albrecht and BillBerry Farms.

Printed in China by Oceanic Graphic Printing

Sometimes Massively Distributed by P.G.W.

Dedication

by S.T. Oner

"Nothing is more destructive of respect for the government and the law of the land than passing laws which cannot be enforced." — Albert Einstein

As always, I wholeheartedly dedicate this book to the fine people at NORML and everyone who has fought against the unjust war on this incredible plant. Though sometimes the fight for legalization of cannabis seems to be endless, rest assured that thanks to the tireless efforts of organizations like NORML we are moving, slowly but surely, towards a more tolerant and rational drug policy in this country.

Following the success of the first three books in this series, *Cannabis Indica: The Essential Guide to the World's Finest Marijuana Strains, Volume 1* and *Volume 2* and *Cannabis Sativa: The Essential Guide to the World's Finest Marijuana Strains, Volume 1,* my thanks must go out to everyone who has been involved in any small part of this project. Every step along this journey brings up new breeders, growers and enthusiasts who contribute their fantastic skills and their abiding love for the plant, allowing this series of books to constantly improve.

Once again, without the fantastic breeders and seed companies whose work appears between these pages, I would never have been able to accomplish such a mammoth task. This book features breeders from the USA, Canada, Holland, Britain, Spain, Denmark, Chile, South Africa, Russia, Slovenia, Chile and quite a few other countries which cannot be listed due to certain draconic laws against this most holy of plants.

There are some contributors who wish to remain anonymous, but who deserve recognition and respect nonetheless, as does everyone on the online forums, especially the people at Breedbay.co.uk, Meduser.ca, Seedfinder.eu and Riotseeds.nl.

Finally I must thank the growers, breeders and writers who inspired me to learn more about this incredible plant; Ed Rosenthal, Jason King, Danny Danko, Mel Thomas, Mel Frank, Greg Green, Grubbycup Stash, Jeff Mowta, Matt Mernagh, Nico Escondido, Jorge Cervantes and The Rev are some big ones, and of course the unforgettable Jack Herer, may he rest in peace. These guys are true trailblazers and their tireless efforts not only set me on my first steps forward on this wonderful journey, but also keep me balanced throughout it. I feel that *Cannabis Sativa, Vol. 2* is a true representation of the variety of cannabis genetics in existence today, and were it not for the hard work and effort of everyone featured in it, it would not exist at all. For this, I say thank you.

Contents

Preface

Cannabis Sativa: An Essential Plant

It's a delight for me to be here once again, presenting you with 100 more of the finest Cannabis Sativa strains to be found in the grow ops and stash bags of marijuana fans today.

As lately as just a few years ago, the wonderful Cannabis Sativa seemed to many to be living in the shadow of her sister, Cannabis Indica. In North America at least, Kush strains ruled the roost to the extent that any weed you got was termed as "some killer Kush, man" by the dealers. Young potheads all over the nation found themselves glued to couches making their way through boxes of Pepperidge Farm products not knowing that there could be another way. Indica-dominant hybrids multiplied at a fantastic rate, while sativa hybrids fell by the wayside, relegated to the 'free seeds' pile at seed banks the world over. Sativa was most definitely pushed out of the limelight while Indica enjoyed its double decade of fame.

Of course, there was a very good reason for this. Advances in indoor grow technology over a number of years had brought marijuana cultivation into the homes of many smokers who had previously been relegated to either buying their favorite herb from that strange guy at the end of the street or throwing some seeds into the ground of a sketchy guerilla grow spot and praying that their beans popped. Those whose beans did pop then had to pray that the plants wouldn't reach the heady heights that some Sativas can grow to and surpass the protective shadow of the plants around them, exposing themselves to both cops and thieves. For many, this was just too much effort and too much of a risk, leaving them trudging back to that same strange

Preface

guy and buying substandard, same-y pot with heavy hearts.

Indoor grow technology changed all this, and suddenly that teeny tiny space under the stairs in your dorm could be turned into a mini grow op without overheating and possibly setting the place on fire and getting yourself a very stern talking to from both your parents and the Dean. That basement, too, or even the walk-in cupboard; all were potential spaces in which to grow your own safe, healthy marijuana, away from prying eyes and thieving hands.

Of course, this forced a turn in the types of marijuana that were being grown the most in the USA. The Cannabis Indica plant is well known for its short, bushy structure and ability to stay squat when necessary; the tall, striking Sativas that look so fantastic outdoors weren't exactly perfect for these new, smaller grow spaces. Those of us who've grown over the years might be expert in coaxing and bending plants to fit less than perfect rooms, but no amount of Low Stress Training can make a 14-foot Lemon Haze monster fit into a cupboard under the stairs. No; for these new indoor growers, Indicas ruled the roost and Kush strains penetrated the market for a good long while.

Thankfully, even through this period of relative unpopularity, Cannabis Sativa retained a hardcore group of supporters in the growers, breeders and cannabis connoisseurs who admired both its high and its beautiful growing traits, as well as the older potheads who had been enjoying it since the 70s and weren't about to change the type of weed in their stash just because a bunch of kids liked something else. Strains such as Lemon Thai by Dutch Flowers and Diesel, now available from Dinafem Seeds and many other seed companies, had inspired a whole generation of Americans to "turn on, tune in and drop out" and they weren't about to turn their back on their favorite genotype just to smoke themselves into a couchlock and watch *Beavis and Butthead*.

It's thanks to this core fanbase that now, while we're enjoying a resurgence of Cannabis Sativa strains due to more and more people being able to grow for medical reasons outdoors, such classic strains are available as seeds once more. If it hadn't been for these growers, we might not be able to enjoy such strains as Sour Lemon OG by Emerald Triangle Seeds and Diesel Ryder by Canada's The Joint Doctor. When certain cannabis varieties fall out of favor, there's always the danger that the genetics might wither away and never be found again. It's a testament to the love that Sativa strains command that many of the best strains from 40 years ago are now back on the market and finding new fans every day.

It was an old hippy grower from Oregon who nursed my own Sativa love back in my rookie toker days. Though I first discovered Sativa strains while working for a marine biologist in the heat of Venezuela, I returned to America not long after with a hungry heart and a determination to grow myself some strains as fantastic as those I'd experienced in the land of Angel Falls and Hugo Chavez. Whilst driving through rural Oregon one spring morning I stopped to have a coffee and a smoke and got chatting to a local when he admired the smell of the last of the South American pot that I'd managed to bring with me. Over a pastry and a bowl we shared our thoughts on the most exotic strains we'd tasted, and he confided in me about his personal grow operation not far away. His property was just a short drive away, though it was seemingly in the middle of nowhere and when we got there, his level of understatement became clear; his "little hobby" was in fact a yard full of 12-foot Sativa plants that carried more vigor and potential than any I've ever seen. Foxtailing buds and colas longer than my arms reached up into the sky over twice my height, as if they were trying to grab the clouds and part them. I'd smoked Sativas but never seen them, and the strange

Preface

beauty of this man's crop had me enthralled. I ended up working on his plants for a season, helping out while he struggled with a bad back and hands that didn't want to do the fiddly work any more. That season gave me a lesson in outdoor Sativa growing that I'll never forget, and tending to those babies with the sun on my back and the fresh Oregon air in my lungs was one of the simplest, happiest times in my life.

It's easy to understand why such hippy happiness is inextricably tied to Sativa plants for people who were around in the 70s. Yet even now, if you gather the world's best breeders in one room and ask them what their absolute favorite strains are, I'll bet that the vast majority will name a Sativa strain. It's not just the soaring, energetic high that garners such love; the challenges that some Sativa strains pose to even the most experienced of growers is a source of inspiration for many. Just as the most complex of classic novels inspire hoards of fans and are revered through the ages, so too do the more complex cannabis strains. Bringing that initial Sativa clone to maturity and bringing down your first huge colas is an experience that no grower forgets, as it influences the way they grow for the rest of their lives.

And yet Sativa cultivation isn't the expert's game it once was. Sativa-dominant hybrids now bring together the ease of growing of Indica strains with the creative, exciting high that everyone loves. Strains such as Sour OG from 420Clones.com and Flo from DJ Short have marginally more Sativa influence that they do Indica, bringing a simpler sort of growing style to each strain, which in turn means that even newbie growers can grow these plants without much struggle. This meshing together of the two main types of cannabis has allowed even small-space growers to add Sativa strains to their grow rooms, and plants like Speed Devil from Sweet Seeds and Kabala from Seeds of Life have even gone as far as to bring ruderalis genetics into the mix,

making sativa-dominant strains more accessible than they ever have been before.

It's thrilling for me to introduce younger smokers and growers to the joys of this plant, and to enjoy a moment of reflection with older enthusiasts when we consider the great times that Sativa strains have brought us over the years. Cannabis Sativa has become essential to my life in many ways as I get older and inevitably less full of the lovable naivety of youth. No longer do I want to swig back energy drinks and party through the night; now a bowl of Diesel and a strong coffee are my "uppers" of choice, and though an Indica will help me relax at the end of a long and busy day, the creative stimulation necessary to make these increasingly popular books always comes from a bong hit of Sativa and a fond memory of that Oregon grow op that started my love affair with this most fabulous plant.

– S.T. Oner

Introduction

The Glory Days of Haze: How I Came to Love Sativa
By Mel Thomas

In the early 80s I was living in London. Those were the Dark Ages for European cannabis users, as all that was readily available was hashish, predominantly some-thing called Moroccan "soap bar," which I never come across these days but appar-ently is still available. There was also a soft and pliable black hash of dubious Afghan origin, as well as a nasty, thinly pressed Lebanese variety known as "flat pack." They were probably best described as what smoking an old rubber car tire would be like. There was occasionally some decent hashish available if you knew the right people, but it was expensive. The only herbal cannabis available at that time was a *Cannabis sativa* strain known as "Jamaican weed," obviously imported from Jamaica. It was compressed into flat slabs that were usually just over a kilo in weight and of very poor quality, full of seeds, with a musty smell. It was quite often slightly moldy from insuf-ficient drying; probably similar to low-grade Mexican "brick weed." If you were buying kilos of Jamaican weed from importers you would be given two or three ounces as a sample; it was so cheap and unpopular that they couldn't give it away.

One of the early pioneers of European cannabis cultivation was Wernard Bruining, who had traveled to America in 1978 and, having seen how the growers there were cultivating high-quality sinsemilla crops, managed to persuade a guy known as "Old Ed" (1916–2007) to travel to Europe and educate us. Over the next five years Old Ed lived with Wernard in Amsterdam, where they founded what became known as the "Green Team" and developed classic hybrids such as Purple Haze, which is said to have been produced from Mexican, Colombian and Thai sativa varieties crossed with

Introduction

an early Dutch indica Skunk. Sacred Seeds bred the original Haze in the late 70s from a combination of several plants including the Mexican, Colombian, Thai and South Indian sativas. Haze is still available today and although it has a long flowering time and below average yield, it has a taste and effect second to none and is definitely one to recommend for those who wish to experience a pure sativa high. Purple Haze #1 is a sativa-dominant variety that I would also recommend to anyone interested in this original Haze strain, as the addition of indica genes has reduced the flowering time and its potency level comes in at a massive 22% THC.

Wernard and Old Ed also came up with the innovative idea of selling seeds, fertilizers and an accompanying instruction leaflet in a cardboard box for 25 Dutch guilders, the aim being to encourage people to start growing their own cannabis plants. The idea caught on and by the mid to late 80s smokers across the Netherlands and Europe began cultivating their own cannabis. Around 1985, Wernard was just setting up the first grow shop, called Positronics, in the Netherlands. This grow shop went on to become the Positronics Seed Company which you can find within these pages with the aforementioned Purple Haze #1 strain. Home cultivation was in its infancy at that time, and myself and a couple of friends decided to do some traveling and we ended up in Hong Kong, of all places. We didn't think too much of the place, but after a couple of days met up with a slightly mad Australian guy. I asked him if he could score us some hash or weed and he shook his head, informing me that it was dangerous trying to get anything like that where we were, but he recommended we go to Thailand. He was an interesting guy and had a wonderful Australian accent; it's similar to our London accent, probably because they transported half of London's working class there in the 1700s. "You should try Thailand, mate: beautiful women and the best weed money can buy." Two days later we were in Bangkok. On the second night we set off on a mission to find some Thai weed. Looking back now, I can see that we were greener than the grass we wanted to score: very young and extremely naive. I didn't even know that there were two types of cannabis plant, indica and sativa, but the Thais are decent people, Buddhists and generally well natured, so we weren't in much danger.

We hit the red-light district of Soi Cowboy and it wasn't long before a young Thai came up and asked us if we wanted girls. I told him we wanted grass, marijuana. He looked around and then, nodding his head quickly, said, "Come." I did the deal with him in a stinking back alley off the main strip, giving him some Thai baht, the local currency, in return for a folded up piece of newspaper he had pulled out from the front of his pants. I was so paranoid I didn't even check it. Feeling very vulnerable, but extremely pleased with ourselves, we found a tuk-tuk taxi and quickly high-tailed it back to the cheap hotel we had found on the Sukhumvit Road, delighted with our illicit stash. It was pure *Cannabis sativa:* Thai buds, fairly dry with quite a few seeds in there and to be honest we thought it didn't look very good at all – that is until we smoked our first bowl on a makeshift pipe we fashioned from an old pen sleeve and some aluminum foil. We had no experience of what good *Cannabis sativa* was like and probably had about two bowls each before we started tripping hard on a psychedelic sativa high. It was just amazing. I have never laughed so much in my born days; every time I looked at my friend John I just doubled over in a giggling fit, and he was the same whenever he looked at me. It was a truly monumental cannabis experience and I never forgot it. We smoked the whole lot and to this day I have no idea how much we had; it was just a big handful of the best Thai grass I've ever smoked. We stayed in Thailand until we ran out of money, but managed to collect quite a few seeds from the stashes that we purchased and smuggled them back to Europe, which was crazy really, but cannabis seeds are not illegal in the UK.

By this point I was a confirmed connoisseur of the *Cannabis sativa* plant; I had discovered that it has more of an uplifting high than indica plants, which tend to have a more sedative effect on the user. One of the first outdoor crops I grew in the UK was composed of several enormous Thai female plants that came from the batch of seeds we had brought back from our travels. It wasn't a great success; they tried their best but produced very spindly flowers and took far too long to finish, meaning that the resultant buds were just no comparison to the cannabis we had purchased in Thailand. Pure *Cannabis sativa* plants need a lengthy and sunny grow season and are not well suited to Northern Europe. Hybrid varieties that contain *Cannabis indica* phenotypes, however, perform well and I had quite a bit of early success with a sativa-dominant strain I acquired from Canada known as Niagara, a mostly-sativa strain that finishes earlier than pure sativa and is fairly mold resistant. Frisian Dew was another variety I found particularly well suited for European outdoor cultivation; this strain is also predominantly sativa and once again fairly mold resistant. Author Jeff Ditchfield reports very heavy yields when these strains are cultivated in Spain, where the climate is particularly suited to outdoor growing. Serious Seeds produce some very reliable sativa-dominant strains that have always performed well outdoors, both here and in North America, particularly Kali Mist by Serious Seeds which I'm pleased to see is

Introduction

featured in this book. It is, in my humble opinion, one of the top sativa-dominant strains available today. It is 90% *Cannabis sativa;* the 10% indica genetics just give it the edge over pure sativas and it retains the classic, tall sativa shape with very few leaves. This allows sunlight to penetrate right through to the lower branches, allowing underside buds to fully develop. I have found this strain also works really well in both greenhouse grows and indoor setups. AK-47 from Serious Seeds is also another dependable, mostly-sativa, high-yielding variety. These plants have a shorter flowering period and produce tight compact buds that are easy to manicure as they are not too leafy. The THC content is high and as the name suggests it is a powerful, hard-hitting plant. Pure Thai varieties are still available and if you have the climate or suitable indoor grow space and wish to try this connoisseurs' variety I would recommend you do so. Those who wish to try a sativa-dominant hybrid that I have actually grown myself should try the classic Lemon Thai by Dutch Flowers, which is also featured in this book. It is a really interesting cross of a pure Thailand sativa with a Hawaiian sativa/indica hybrid variety and gives good yields indoors and finishes in around 9 weeks.

In America during the 70s the herbal cannabis available came predominantly from countries producing *Cannabis sativa,* such as Mexico and Colombia. The founder of *High Times* magazine, Tom Forcade, was reputedly involved in smuggling planeloads of Colombian sativa into the U.S., where it was known as Colombia Gold, Panama Red, or Acapulco Gold. Attempts to grow pure *Cannabis sativa* strains with seeds from these varieties proved to give variable results, as the growing season even in California was less suitable than Colombia's. It wasn't until the introduction of *Cannabis indica* genetics, predominantly from Afghanistan, that breeders were able to produce strains with shorter flowering times that were suitable for both outdoor growing in the North American climate and indoor cultivation when the use of horticultural lighting became more widespread. The Afghan indicas were hybridized with the pure *Cannabis sativa* varieties from Colombia and Mexico.

There has always been a gulf between those that enjoy growing sativa plants and those that enjoy growing indicas, due to their very different characteristics as well as their different highs. Sativa plants are taller than indicas; they grow very quickly and can reach heights of 20 feet in a single season, yet despite having narrower leaves, sativa strains contain more accessory pigments, which are light-absorbing compounds that work in conjunction with chlorophyll. A pigment is any substance that absorbs light and the color of the pigment comes from the wavelengths of light not absorbed,

Introduction

which it reflects, and is why we see plants as green in color. Sativa plants have less chlorophyll content than indicas, and chlorophyll residue is what gives incorrectly dried cannabis bud its "green" taste and explains why sativas are said to have a better aftertaste than many indica strains: there is simply less chlorophyll to remove in the drying process. Flavors from correctly dried and cured *Cannabis sativa* flowers range from earthy to sweet and fruity.

There seems to be a great deal of misinformation written about the use of *Cannabis sativa* varieties for indoor cultivation and some of what's written can be very misleading. It's true that pure sativas will grow tall and stretch, but this doesn't mean you can't use them indoors; they can be controlled even by a novice gardener. You just have to be quite ruthless with your pruning and train the branches. If space really is an issue in your grow area then opt for a sativa hybrid as the addition of indica genetics produces a more compact plant. Given optimum conditions pure *Cannabis sativas* can grow faster and yield more than many indicas. The buds are just less dense.

Cannabis sativa strains suffered from waning popularity in the 90s as indica strains became more popular. However, there is now a new resurgence of interest in the plant and this is mainly due to the sativa varieties having higher THC content as opposed to CBD levels. THC gives an uplifting, cerebral type of high, leaving the user feeling more energetic and stimulating brain activity to a far greater extent than CBD. Indica Skunk-type strains tend to have higher concentrations of CBD and can leave the user "couch locked," whereas the higher THC content in sativa strains produces a euphoric, almost mildly hallucinogenic effect, without some of the negative feelings that can be associated with heavy indica use, such as lethargy and occasionally paranoia. It seems like the new smokers of today are looking for the same high their parents had back in the 70s – the one that I've always enjoyed, too. I was delighted to be asked to write a short introduction for this book as I am a huge fan of *Cannabis sativa* strains and all of the varieties you find profiled in here are wonderful examples of this amazing plant. I hope you enjoy reading it as much as I did and are encouraged to experiment with these superb sativa varieties.

Shiva bless.

SATIVA
The Strains

Although this strain sounds like what Michael Jackson might have smoked backstage in his "I Want You Back" years, it's actually a fantastic African-Pakistani strain created by the killer team of Tropical Seeds Company and CannaBioGen. Together, these two Spanish breeding powerhouses have harnessed the best qualities of a Swazi Polokwane plant and a Purple Chitral F1 straight from the hills of Pakistan.

AfroKush's Polokwane Swazi mother plant brings a very compact structure which finishes in around 80-85 days with a very decent yield. Though this is fast for a sativa-dominant strain, it's still longer than indica strains, so You'll Wanna Be Startin' Somethin' as soon as you get your hands on these seeds so you don't have to wait around for that first smoke! These plants do best with a lot of light, so if there Ain't No Sunshine where you live, consider growing indoors. Nearer harvest time, the resin stacks in layers on the buds and the flowers form neat colas that mean your plant will look anything but Bad!

Tropical Seeds Company and CannaBioGen, Spain

Sativa-Dominant

Genetics: Swazi Polokwane x Purple Pakistan Chitral F1

tropicalseedscompany.com

facebook.com/ TropicalSeeds

cannabiogen.com

The high of AfroKush is a very fast-hitting, playful sort of experience that will make the time fly and will almost always be Gone Too Soon, so make sure you've got a nice fat stash to keep you Off The Wall all day long. Just Don't Stop Til You Get Enough!

Amazing Haze

I think Holland's Homegrown Fantaseeds (still love that name, guys – good work) must have had a laugh when they named this strain. In the same way that calling a strain "Dope Kush" or "Killer Diesel" is bound to cause some confusion amongst those smoking it, Amazing Haze's name practically guarantees that tokers will have a hard time explaining to their equally stoned friends what got them so ripped. We can't really call them out for being misleading, though, as this Amnesia Haze x Caramella cross really is amazing, and any grower will tell you that it's Haze through and through. I guess it's a great name after all!

Amazing Haze may not be the best strain for newbies, but those with a few grows under their belt will find her very enjoyable to cultivate. The flowering time sits at the longer end of the spectrum, averaging 11 or 12 weeks, but all your hard work will pay off in spades, with phenomenally resinous buds that smell like flowers.

A taste like caramel popcorn will give way to a high that's pure Amnesia Haze; it takes your brain out, switches it around, and puts it back in the other way. You won't remember what strain you're smoking, or where you are, or what smoking even is, but as they say, ignorance is bliss – and Amazing Haze certainly is blissful!

Homegrown Fantaseeds, Holland

Sativa-Dominant

Genetics: Amnesia Haze x Caramella

Potency: THC 19%

homegrownfantaseeds.com

Angel's Breath

Here's a fact for you: Mr. Nice's autobiography is the one single book that all stoners have read. You can strike up a conversation over a joint in any country anywhere in the world, and regardless of your new friend's gender, race or location, at some point he or she will bring up Mr. Nice. They even made a movie of the book, just for pot-heads, starring that Welsh guy from Notting Hill whose name no one can say. With such fame, then, Mr. Nice has a lot to live up to with his strains – and he doesn't disappoint his bookish, film-watching fans one little bit. Created by breeders Nevil and Shantibaba, Angel's Breath is an impressive cross between two distinct Haze plants, one Mango and one from Afghanistan, which comprises Skunk and Northern Lights #5 heritage and therefore commands as much attention as Mr. Nice himself.

Parent strain Mango Haze is a favorite over at Mr. Nice Seeds, as they consider it to be their highest achieving plant since the Super Silver Haze that set the market on fire back in the late 90s. As its offspring, Angel's Breath is always going to be impressive, although if you're short on patience and a little highly strung, you might want to stick with buying this one from your local dispensary. Suited more to an experienced grower, this strain has so much Haze influence in its genetics that a flowering time of 11 to 12 weeks is not uncommon. To bring that time down a little, the breeders suggest flowering a clone from the seed mother, a tip that has been noted amongst many growers of this plant. It is also recommended that you only expose the plant to 3 to 4 days of 18-hour light periods, and flip directly into 12/12. Angel's Breath can also be more challenging to look after than other plants, although as with most things, the effort will pay off double when harvest rolls around. Hydro systems can foster this strain very well, and outdoor or greenhouse grows are usually the best choices. An indoor grower can expect yields of 500 grams per square yard of grow space, making this a good commercial strain as well as one that will blow your mind!

Mr. Nice Seedbank, Holland

Sativa-Dominant

Genetics: Mango Haze x Afghan Haze

Potency: THC 20%

mrnice.nl

I'm not a religious person by any stretch of the imagination, but if this is what the angels are smoking then I might have to give this God dude another chance; I didn't realize that eternal salvation would be like a hot-boxed vapor lounge. If they put that on the signs outside churches, I think more people would go – or perhaps they could just waft the amazing fruity smell of this strain in the direction of the sinners. I'm sure they'd all repent, or at least feel like they had!

Arjan's Strawberry Haze

Arjan Roskam is a hell of a lot taller than you'd think. He might seem to be the smallest when he's standing with his Green House Seed Co. friends, but trust me; they're just Dutch giants too. The only thing more intimidating than standing next to this man if you're short on stature and mad high is standing next to him and thinking about what a massive impact he's made on the worldwide cannabis community. Green House Seeds are without a doubt the world's biggest seed company, and they party with people like Snoop Dogg and Woody Harrelson when they visit Amsterdam. All this seems very Lady Gaga until you remember that they also pioneered the idea of color-coded seeds and continue to create strains that become instantly recognizable and much sought after.

Arjan's Strawberry Haze is one of these strains; if you mention the name around a group of stoners they'll all nod and start pontificating about whether it does really taste like strawberries or not. They probably won't know, however, that it was created from a Swiss sativa plant crossed with a Northern Lights #5 Haze Mist. As such, your Arjan's Strawberry Haze plants will exhibit typical sativa-style growth with long, expansive branches that look as if they're trying to hug the whole crop. This strain, like its skyscraper breeder dad, does have a tendency to stretch, so be sure to keep your lights as close to the plants as possible without burning them in order to minimize stretching (though I wouldn't try the same with Arjan himself). This strain really enjoys hot climates and can manage in temperate ones, although it won't be the happiest it could be. It's ideal for a ScrOG set up, and will respond very well to Low Stress Training. Your plants should be finished fully in 10 weeks in an indoor grow and give up to 600 grams per square yard of grow room; a pretty sizable yield for any indoor grower! A breeder's tip is to allow flowering for one extra week, just to really bring out the plant's fantastic flavor. Outdoor cultivators can expect to harvest in the middle of October with a gigantic yield of up to 800 grams per plant; now that's a strain for commercial cultivation if I ever saw one!

Green House Seed Co., Holland
Sativa-Dominant
Genetics: Swiss Sativa x NL5 Haze Mist
Potency: THC 19.72%
greenhouseseeds.nl

If you ever do find yourself next to the "King of Cannabis" for whatever reason, his own Strawberry Haze might be the perfect strain to smoke. After the thick smoke (which may or may not taste just like strawberries, depending on your taste buds) clears, you'll be hit with a confident, creative and social stone, and you may even get up the nerve to chat with the big man himself before breaking down in fits of giggles and telling him how much you love his shit.

Cannabis Sativa The Essential Guide to the World's Finest Marijuana Strains, Volume 2

Atomic +

Spain's North of Seeds have become well known in Europe and further abroad for their fantastic dedication to detail and customer service, going out of their way to ensure that their seeds reach their customers in the best possible conditions. In an Internet age when everyone is on forums, word spreads quickly, and thanks to their business style as well as their great strains, North of Seeds are a grower's favorite company these days. Their legion of fans will no doubt be thrilled with this strain, an enigmatic sativa-dominant plant that's a heavy yielder but isn't a nightmare to grow.

As a heavy sativa-dominant strain, Atomic + is a large plant that's most used to growing outdoors. Despite this, it can also been grown indoors with some good training and pre-planning to keep you ahead of the game. There is a good deal of stretch in this plant, so be sure to keep your lights as close to the plants as possible when growing indoor to minimize the additional stretch as much as possible. This can be a good choice for a ScROG set up. The leaves of Atomic + are pencil thin and so sharp you feel as if you should be wearing a hockey helmet with a half-face visor just to walk around your grow room. As they say, it's all fun and games until someone loses an eye. When flipped into the flowering stage this strain will bloom very rapidly, barely giving mold the time to take hold – but this does mean that your spindly plants might need some extra help from their caregiver towards the time for harvest.

North of Seeds, Spain

Sativa-Dominant

Potency: THC 12-16%

northofseeds.com

In fact, the best way to deal with this is to stake the plants early on in the vegetative stage and then allow them to grow and flower around the stakes that are already there. This will save you from having to wrestle with the plants later on and endanger your soft eyes even more. For indoor growers, the flowering time will be 55 days, whereas outdoor growers can expect to harvest around the 10th of October or just before, depending on when they were planted. While indoor growers can expect their final harvests to weigh in at around 600 grams per square yard of grow space, outdoor growers can expect a little more, with around 650 grams of top bud per plant.

As with all good sativa strains, Atomic + is almost all up in the head. The incredibly stinky buds will smell of wood and citrus, with a distinct lemony aroma cutting through everything else. Once lit, these buds give a nice thick smoke that rushes up your nose and gives your brain a cuddle, a tickle and a bit of a back massage all at the same time. Ignore the fact that this ill-considered metaphor results in some sort of 4-armed marijuana beast pummeling and squishing you in all sorts of ways, and just enjoy the high!

Auto AK-47 x Auto Hindu Kush

The UK's Lowlife Seeds must be huge fans of the Joint Doctor, as they specialize in creating strains that encompass the auto-flowering traits that he first brought to the market. The British part of me says that this is because there just isn't enough sun in the UK to grow normal plants, but I know that in actual fact these guys are doing amazing work with a relatively new variety of cannabis plants and so they deserve a lot of respect! This plant is a cross that started out as an experiment (as all the best things in life do), which turned out to be just what they were after, with a balanced blend of Kush and AK-47 genetics and a hint of ruderalis to keep things auto.

This strain worked out so well that the Lowlife breeders added it quickly to their catalog of auto-flowering F1 strains. This is a particularly good strain for anyone looking to move into sativa cultivation if they're also short on space, as it will not grow beyond 2 feet tall but still gives an amazing sativa-dominant high when smoked. Your Auto AK-47 x Auto Hindu Kush plant will exhibit good branching and will get bushier and bushier as it reaches the end of the flowering stage; in fact, you might have some difficulty even finding the branches when it's time to harvest. This strain finishes completely in 10 weeks from seed and with the right conditions you'll see speedy growth right from the second the taproot pops. As well as a small indoor grow space, this strain can be good for outdoor and greenhouse grows, though my preference for autos is always indoors! The finished buds will be very, very resinous; so much so that they'll look too sticky to touch. When you do grab ahold of them you'll be surprised how weighty they are. Be sure to dry them properly to avoid bud rot!

Lowlife Seeds, UK

Sativa-Dominant

Genetics: Auto AK-47 x Auto Hindu Kush

Potency: THC 15%

seedsman.com

lowlifeseeds.com

Due to the hybrid nature of this plant, the high is a layered, interesting one. The buds will give off a Kushy smell tempered with a little spiciness, and when you blaze them up you'll find that the hard-hitting traits of the AK-47 have come through to the offspring, though the effects are more balanced than with the parent plants. This mixed head and body high, with a good dose of couch lock, makes Auto AK-47 x Auto Hindu Kush a superb strain for sitting with your buddies all day, talking smack and smoking even more bud.

Bandana

I've always thought that they should name strains after fashion faux-pas that I've made in my life, and as they won't be calling a strain Seriously Patchy Pants or Lame Cowboy Hat any time soon I think Bandana is the closest I'm going to get. Either AlphaKronik Genes knew me when I was a punk teenager or they made the same mistakes themselves; either way, they've created a killer strain from a 707 Headband female clone and a Snowdawg BX male that will make some of us think of our glory days – and our less than glorious days too!

Based in the U.S., AlphaKronik are a new-school company who have a phenomenal variety of genetics and aren't afraid to do interesting things with them. Bandana is one of their newest strains, as it was released in late 2011, and is only limited edition for now – so if you get the chance to buy some beans, don't let them slip through your hands.

The Headband parent is known for its basketball-player-huge stature and skunk taste, while the Snowdawg pop sweetens out the bitterness in the smoke and brings some strength and resilience to the actual plant. However, it would take a lot of indica genetics to really tame the Headband growth patterns and as such, Bandana will end up as a big ol' plant unless you take measures to keep her down! When planting your seeds or clones, you should be sure to leave a lot of room for its accelerated growth patterns. Though she'll coast along nicely through the vegetative stage, in the early stages of flowering your plant can triple its size – that's right, triple! Between the first and last weeks of flowering your plant can change so much you barely recognize it, kinda like the main 3 kids in the first and last Harry Potter movies: who are these rough-looking yuppies and where did those infants go?.

AlphaKronik Genes, USA

Sativa-Dominant

Genetics: 707 Headband x Snowdawg BX

Potency: THC 17%

basilbush.co.uk

facebook.com/ AlphaKronik

All this may seem like a lot of fuss, but growing sativa plants is always ultimately rewarding, and Bandana is no different. The medical marijuana community especially will love this strain, as it holds a lot of potential benefits for them. Any patients suffering from uncontrollable movements such as spasms will find it a great help, and it may also be effective in preventing seizures for some. It is also great medicine for those with joint and muscle pains, as well as patients suffering from MS, Crohn's disease and cerebral palsy. For the rest of us, Bandana brings a great energetic, chatty vibe with a nice smooth release – making it easy to forget about the Fashion Dark Ages we all went through.

Biddy Early

This strain was first developed by the awesome Magus Genetics and is now being produced by the equally awesome Serious Seeds. No matter who's producing it, though, this is a really interesting combination of Early Pearl x Skunk and Warlock genetics; they should have called it Warlock Skunk for maximum comedic effect, but let's not quibble over that.

As Magus's first outdoor strain this was something of an experiment, but one that turned out fantastically. With typical sativa outdoor growth it can reach 7 feet with ease, and will exhibit the Christmas-tree shape that makes sativas so recognizable. Biddy Early can also be grown indoors, although clone mothers have a strong tendency to start flowering even under 18 hours of light, so be sure to keep her under 24 hours of light. The flowering period sits at 9 weeks, and during this time most of the plants will exhibit red and purple colorings if exposed to colder temperatures which is great for bag appeal.

Biddy Early's finished buds will be reddish-orange and will smell like overripe fruit or seriously sugary candies. When the smooth smoke clears the powerful, energetic high will take over your head, stimulating you in all the right places and making you into a social powerhouse. This is definitely one for the evening, not a morning wake 'n bake!

Developed by Magus Genetics; now produced by Serious Seeds, Holland

Sativa-Dominant

Genetics: (Early Pearl x Skunk) x Warlock

seriousseeds.com

Black Light

No, this is not the quintessential acid-fiend's bedroom illumination, but rather a fantastic strain from America's M.G.M. Genetics (who, as far as I know, are not related to either the film studios or the casino). M.G.M. are a great medical collective who have consistently impressed me by pulling rare and interesting genetics out of their pocket like other people pull out candy. They've done this yet again with this strain, which is a mix of a Massachusetts heritage cut of Northern Lights and a male plant of The Black, a 90% indica strain from B.C. Bud Depot. This project began at the request of a patient, who asked the breeders to create a Haze-dominant sativa strain with a mild, sweet flavor that was also easy to grow, and quick flowering. Not only did this patient tap in to the unknown desires of 90% of sativa lovers with that request, but he also started the M.G.M. breeders on the path to creating one of my favorite new strains.

After the breeders found the phenotype that they liked best, Black Light was back-crossed to stabilize it and ensure that it produces good seeds. As per the original request, it is a very simple plant to grow, needing only a simple soil set up and some basic fertilizer in the flowering stage to get the very best out of her. Topping is very necessary, as it will quickly overtake your grow room and sign over the deeds to your house to itself unless you're careful. Topping will keep it tame but still producing well. In this set up, Black Light will be fully finished in 9 weeks. However, if you grow in hydro then you're in for a real treat; with only 3 weeks of vegetative growth and regular topping you can expect absolutely gargantuan yields of premium bud. In this type of set up, each plant will need at least 6 feet of space to grow into, and they will stretch, no matter what you do. Topping will be your go-to technique again, especially if you accidentally veg it for too long! Treating Black Light with molasses in the final 2 weeks of flowering will help to bring out a super sweet, slightly smoky taste that is like thick black toffee – a real treat!

M.G.M. Genetics, USA

Sativa-Dominant

Genetics: The Black x Northern Lights (Massachusetts Heritage Cut)

Potency: THC 26%

The mild, sweet flavor that the patient asked for is definitely there in the Black Light smoke, along with a nutty, carroty undertone and a very sweet smell. The high is pure Haze: all cerebral, very confusing and guaranteed to make you hungry. By the time you come around you'll probably find yourself standing at a hot dog stall wearing nothing but a T-shirt and no pants – but you'll feel really great about that.

Blueshade

It's a mystery to me that Danish seed companies aren't more widely loved, as I've always had great experiences with strains from the country of good bacon and big floppy dogs. Both Dane Strains and Zenseeds have produced some fantastic varieties, and Dane Strains have a beautifully unique plant in this sativa-dominant strain, Blueshade.

Usually when you come across new cannabis hybrids, you know a little bit about at least one of the parent strains. When I first found Blueshade and learned of its origins, I had absolutely no idea what either of them were. I've since learned that Blueshade is a cross between a phenomenal Danish strain that can be grown outdoors even in the harsh weather of Denmark called Night Shade, and Blue Streak from Mdanzig. Blue Streak is a very interesting strain, as it comprises genetics from DJ Short's famous Blueberry, the Joint Doctor's Lowryder and Dutch Passion's Master Kush. Such a combination on its own would necessitate some serious respect, but when coupled with a strain that's apparently hardier than a Bang & Olufsen sound system, it's going to cause some serious waves!

Dane Strains, Denmark

Sativa-Dominant

Genetics: Blue Streak x Night Shade

Potency: THC 21%

cannaseeds.dk

As this plant is in the Blueberry lineage, it will show those gorgeous purpley-blue tones that everyone knows and loves in the later stages of flowering. If you're keen for your final buds to be bluer than some frostbitten fingers, then be sure to expose them to a little cold air; this will bring the violet tones right out (and, incidentally, give your nugs a higher street value). The Blueberry grandparent also brings a very sturdy structure to this plant, so it should be very capable of holding its own weight all the way through to harvest time. The presence of Lowryder in the family tree also means that Blueshade is an autoflowering strain, so it doesn't need a change in light cycle to move from the vegetative to the flowering stages; it will just go when it's ready. This, along with the plant's hardiness, means if you live in a more temperate country and have an outdoor guerilla grow that you can't tend to that often, Blueshade might just be the strain that you've been looking for.

Though the yield isn't as massive as other sativa strains, Blueshade nugs are well worth the minimal effort it takes to grow them. The high is a perfect balance of head and body high, and is mild enough for rookie tokers to enjoy it without feeling like they're going to somehow fall off the floor. Another strain to make Denmark proud.

Brainstorm Haze

Delta 9 Labs have been kicking around in the cannabis world for some time now, and they've received a lot of respect from the wider community due to their commitment to growing all their seeds organically. They also have been pumping out amazing strains as if it's no effort whatsoever, including one of my favorites, Mekong Haze.

Brainstorm Haze is a definite contender for that title now though, as it brings together genetics from a Pure Thai Haze sativa mother and Delta 9's own Stargazer, which is a Sensi Star, Warlock and AK-47 cross.

This strain is a perfect one for indoor cultivation, and will take 12 weeks to finish in a properly controlled environment. It can also be grown outdoors if that's your preference, although the breeders recommend warmer climates and southern latitudes for optimum results. The plants will be tall in either situation, and will enjoy guano fertilizers with high nitrogen.

Your Brainstorm Haze yield will be as huge as it is impressive, and the smoke, as you might imagine, will set you off on a creative streak that might never end.

Delta 9 Labs, Holland

Sativa-Dominant

Genetics: Pure Thai Haze x Stargazer

Potency: THC 16-20%

delta9labs.com

Cannatonic

Spain's Resin Seeds may have been in business for only a few years, but their head breeder is a veteran of Spain's cannabis community, having owned a successful grow shop in Barcelona for many years before. He obviously listened to his customers while he was there, as this cross between MK Ultra F1 and a G-13 Haze plant hits all of a grower's most wanted traits.

Not only does Cannatonic grow like an indica but smell like a sativa, it encompasses genetics of the ubiquitous G-13 plant that was allegedly stolen from a US government grow op back in the day. This is already enough to get growers excited, but coupling this with an ease of growing and a high yield, and you'll have them melting in the palms of your hands (especially if those hands are covered in resin). Cannatonic will finish in 10 weeks indoors with a yield of 500 grams per square yard of grow space, or mid-October outdoors with a yield of 400 grams per plant.

A favorite with medical patients, this strain is fantastic for alleviating chronic pain even for the most needy of patients. I can't tell you any more about the high of this plant than the name can; after a few joints you'll find yourself consumed by the high and unable or unwilling to move out of it. You will truly be Cannatonic.

Resin Seeds, Spain

Sativa-Dominant

Genetics: MK Ultra F1 x G-13 Haze

Potency: THC 6.2%

resinseeds.net

Cheese Tease

I always thought it was the French that were known as the world's best fromage connoisseurs, but in my experience it's always been the British who are mad on the Cheese – the weed strain, that is. Any British breeder worth their salt has a Cheese cross in the works or on the market, and Kaliman Seeds have gone even further with Cheese Tease, using a 1989 Exodus Cheese clone AND a Skunk #1 F1 to make what must be one of the most popular strains available in Britain today; the last time I went to London, Skunk was about all you could get. Any more UK influence and it would be wearing suspenders, eating overcooked meat and listening to The Clash – which, incidentally, is what you might end up doing after you've lit up a sick little nug of this strain. Watch out: the British are coming.

Kaliman Seeds reckon that this strain is a marked improvement on many of the Skunk #1 strains available today, as it has more depth of flavor than other comparable strains. When growing, it will get to a medium height and can be kept from getting too branchy with some basic Low Stress Training. Outdoor growers will be ready to harvest at the end of September, and indoor growers should note the flowering time of 8 to 11 weeks. As with any Skunk-influenced strain, this one is going to be a stinker in the later stages of flowering especially, so design your grow room's ventilation system with this in mind and be sure to use charcoal filters to Clampdown on escaping odors; remember that you're not Joe Cocker, so if someone finds out about your grow and you fight the law, the law is probably going to win. Either way, be sure you Know Your Rights just in case it comes to that – and don't take anyone into your grow room that you don't know. You don't want to give that hot girl Julie a tour of the facility only to find out that Julie's Been Working For The Drug Squad.

Kaliman Seeds, UK

Sativa-Dominant

Genetics: 1989 Exodus Cheese x Skunk #1 F1

Potency: THC 16%

kaliman.co.uk

seedsman.com

Those who found the original Cheese a little too overpowering will love Cheese Tease as the smell is somewhat more subdued but the high is just as killer. You might be under Complete Control of the high, as it creeps up around your brain and sets up camp there, but you shouldn't worry too much; the energy and creativity of this strain ensures that you'll have some Groovy Times. You will feel London Calling as the effects set in, but the furthest you're going to get is the local Walmart in your Brand New Cadillac to buy some treats and Koka Kola – just be sure not to get too confused or you might get Lost In The Supermarket.

ChemDawg (#4 Cut)

I could spend all day here going over the finer points of the ChemDawg folklore, but every self-respecting stoner has heard it all a million times before and I don't want to bore you to sleep before we even get started. Almost every story about the origins of this strain at least agree on one thing; the seeds came from a $500 ounce bought by the breeder, Chemdog, at a Grateful Dead concert at Deer Creek Amphitheatre back in the day. From these shaky beginnings, ChemDawg has since become one of the most sought-after strains in recent history, despite having an unknown lineage that must be sativa-dominant. This version of the variety, from Canada's Dr. Greenthumb, is said to be the famed #4 cut of the original plant; the phenotype that the original seller of the ounce liked the best.

Over the years several theories have sprung up regarding ChemDawg's roots (if you'll pardon the pun). Some say the heritage is an unknown indica strain, while others believe that the plant contains Nepali and Thai sativa genetics. I'm given to believing the second theory more, as it grows in a sativa-dominant way and gives a lovely energizing high. With a strong structure, ChemDawg #4 is a plant that isn't fussy and will be as happy indoors as it will be out. It can get large if you allow it the space to do so, but if you're an indoor grower certain training techniques can also help you to keep your plants at the perfect size. The breeder recommends not topping, as he doesn't, but if you prefer to top your plants you should do so radially, starting at the second node and finishing at the sixth.

Dr. Greenthumb Seeds, Canada

Sativa-Dominant

Potency: THC 21-24%

drgreenthumb.com

When your nugs light up, you'll feel as if you're inhaling some beautiful perfume, but without the overwhelming feeling you get when a woman who has practically bathed in Chanel No. 5 walks by at a party. As with all the most famous strains, Chem-Dawg #4 is a mad heavy hitter and will hit you like a brick wall when you're not looking – so if you find yourself on the floor asking what the hell happened, you might find your answer in the joint you're smoking! However, the sativa prevalence will come through after a little while and you'll feel your mood hugely uplifted and your jelly-like body will be raring to go, even if it can't. It's a little like swimming in molasses; you won't feel like you're going anywhere, but slowly and surely, you are. After a few hours have passed you won't feel sluggish or tired, just inspired; there'll be no doubt in your mind as to why ChemDawg #4 is as magical to the cannabis community as the One Ring is to Frodo Baggins.

ChemDog IX-III x The Killing Fields

If the name of this strain is a little too cumbersome for you, I suggest you just call it That Damn Killer Strain. Ultimate Seeds, purveyors of some very cool genetics, have done it again with this cross between the world's most enigmatic strain and one of the strongest and most interesting sativa-dominant hybrids around.

This cross displays all the typical hybrid vigor in its growth patterns, although it won't grow out of control or too tall to deal with. Despite this, she isn't a plant that's recommended for newbie growers; those with a few years of cultivation behind them will enjoy the challenges that this strain presents and will have the skill to get the most out of it. By the end of the 9-week flowering time, your ChemDog IX-III x Killing Fields plants will be covered in rock hard buds that smell fantastic and look even better.

Ultimate Seeds

Sativa-Dominant

Genetics: ChemDawg x The Killing Fields

Potency: THC 24%

ultimateseeds.com

These plants are high yielding, so your harvest will leave you snowed under with nugs, but do exercise some caution; these tempting buds give an extremely strong and enjoyable high that's very spacy and kills pain for medical users.

Cinderella 99 BX1

With so many new seed companies cropping up these days, it can be difficult for a breeding collective to carve out a place for themselves in such a saturated market. Mosca Seeds have managed to make a name for themselves by stabilizing and perfecting some classic strains, such as this Cinderella 99 backcross. This is the result of breeding together two Cinderella 99 inbred lines, originally from the Brothers Grimm, and backcrossing one generation to bring out the "pineapple" phenotype.

This strain was originally bred to be an indoor crop, but I know a few growers who swear to its ability to grow outdoors too, so it might be more adaptable than first thought. As a mostly sativa strain it will grow to an enormous size when given the fresh air and increased space of an outdoor grow, and my friends have reported huge yields of up to 700 grams that kept them high for about a year! The flowering time sits at around 52 days, although this can vary when grown outdoors. Staking may be necessary nearer to harvest time due to such large yields.

Mosca Seeds

Sativa-Dominant

Genetics: Cinderella 99

seedsman.com

seedbay.com

Cinderella 99 strains are known for being totally delicious, and the taste of this BX will linger with you all day. So will the high, which starts out quite mild then eventually takes over your whole being without even so much as a "Hello." I always knew these princesses were rude.

Clockwork Orange Haze

I am a huge fan of *Clockwork Orange* (the movie, the book, the strain from Riot Seeds and the original vinyl soundtrack) and I am also a huge fan of SinSemilla-Works! from the U.S., so I knew I would love this strain as soon as I heard of it. I might have been wrong in thinking it would somehow involve Malcolm McDowell and milk+, but I was not wrong in thinking that I would love it. A cross between a True Blueberry from DJ Short and an Orange Haze plant, this is a heavy sativa-dominant that's real horrorshow.

Clockwork Orange Haze is a strain that will happily grow in any environment, though outdoor growers will love it especially. As with any Blue strain it will show its colorings best in a colder environment, and as its Blue colorings come out its bag appeal will increase. This is a fast hybrid, finishing in less than 8 weeks, and yielding between 400 and 500 grams per square yard of grow space.

Your soomka of Clockwork Orange Haze buds will be gorgeous, and will make you very popular amongst your droogs. Just a couple of the ol' tokes will make your gulliver fly right off your body, so any veck without a high tolerance should be careful not to smoke too much, or they might end up listening to Beethoven endlessly and drinking too much milk.

PHOTOS BY GIORGIO ALVAREZZO

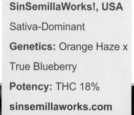

SinSemillaWorks!, USA

Sativa-Dominant

Genetics: Orange Haze x True Blueberry

Potency: THC 18%

sinsemillaworks.com

Cotton Candy

My French friend once told me that cotton candy in France is known as "*barbe à papa*", which literally means "Dad's beard." Once I picked myself up off the floor from laughing I made sure that little gem of information stayed in there, and now every time I meet a French person I enjoy their bewildered looks when I recite the phrase and melt into fits of laughter again. Fantastic.

I'd be a little bewildered if my dad's beard looked like this Cotton Candy, though; seeing my paternal parent with huge lavender colas of top-quality pot springing from his chin might be a bit disconcerting, plus I'd wonder how Delicious Seeds got their awesome strain to grow on such a weathered surface. I wouldn't exactly be surprised, though; this Spanish company are all about surpassing the norm and making great things happen. Their Cotton Candy is a blend of Lavender, which has Skunk, Afghani and Hawaiian heritage, and Power Plant, which is one of the highest-yielding strains from South Africa. This combination is so good on paper that you think it must be something of a disappointment in real life – but trust me, it is most definitely not.

Delicious Seeds, Spain

Sativa-Dominant

Genetics: Lavender x

Power Plant

Potency: THC 20%

deliciousseeds.com

hemppassion.com

facebook.com/

DeliciousSeeds

This dad's beard grows like Gandalf's facial hair, getting very big very quickly and commanding a lot of respect. It's resistant to fungi, mold, pests and stress – as I imagine Gandalf's beard is too – making it a very easy plant to grow, despite its size. It also produces foxtail buds, which I absolutely love, and the high calyx-to-leaf ratio means that at the end of the 70 days, your harvest will be a joy. A grower I know commented that this might be the best-yielding strain he's ever seen, and I think he might just be right. The official stats for production are 550 grams per square yard of indoor grow space and 600 grams per square yard of outdoor grow space, making Cotton Candy a great strain for commercial grow purposes or just for those who smoke a fucking lot of pot.

As you might expect from a strain named after what is basically sugary fuzz, these nugs taste and smell super sweet. In fact, it's so pungent that even having the buds in the room with you will set you off on a mad sugar high before you've even smoked. When you do light up, you'll be as happy as a child at a fairground, and acting the exact same way. Rest assured, next time someone tells me they've got dad's beard I'll be doing less laughing and a lot more salivating – until after the smoke, that is, when I'll be melting into laughter all over again!

Danish Diesel

I'm not sure if the Danish cannabis community has been lying low for the last 30 years or whether I've just been totally ignorant to its existence, but over the last few years it seems that the breeding community in Denmark has gone nuclear. Such great strains are coming from that part of the world, like this Danish Diesel from Sadhu Seeds. This strain came from a Diesel #1 plant that was crossed with a Danish sativa plant to bring Danish strains to the masses!

Though this strain was created in the mid 90s, Sadhu Seeds managed to get hold of a clone from the last batch of the original seeds. They feminized the strain and grew it out, finding that it was very well suited to the Nordic climate thanks to its tolerance to cold. This is a great outdoor strain which is very easy to grow and very resistant to a whole host of fungi. The flowering period is very short, at 7-8 weeks indoors, or 15 September outdoors in the Northern hemisphere.

That unforgettable Diesel smell surrounds these nugs, and the high is pure Diesel too; uplifting, exciting and full of energy. The slightly orange-y taste will sit on the palate almost as long as the high sits on the head, leaving you pleasantly spent, pasted to the couch and singing the Danish national anthem with a tear in your eye.

Sadhu Seeds, Denmark

Sativa-Dominant

Genetics: Diesel #1 x

Danish Sativa

Potency: THC 21%

grobedre.dk

chillo.dk

sadhu-seeds.com

PHOTOS BY GRO BEDRE MAGAZINE

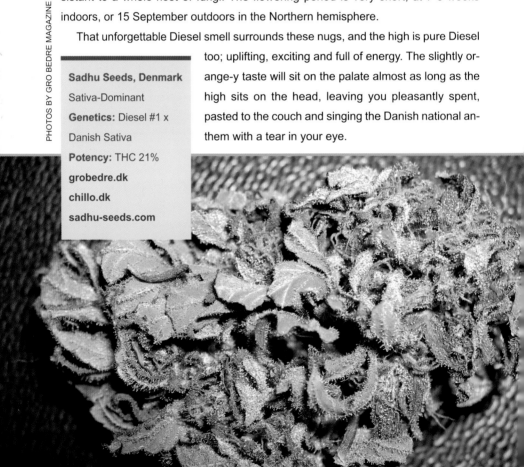

Destroyer x Deep Chunk/Uzbekistan

I have never been to Chile, but when I eventually do get there, I'll for sure be looking up Trip Seeds. Not only do they work with 100% Chilean genetics, but they are also providing great crosses of some already fantastic plants to make even better ones! I'm also sure that they must know where to get the very best Chilean wine, and information like that is nothing to sniff at. Hopefully while we're driving to the vineyard we can enjoy a toke of their Destroyer x Deep Chunk/Uzbekistani cross and chat about Milton Friedman and what he did wrong – though given the potency of this strain, that conversation might just melt into one about pretty trees and shapes instead.

There are three phenotypes of this strain, although the breeders are in the process of picking their favorite so they can then go on and stabilize it. These phenotypes are like triplets: different in a couple of minor ways but largely the same and only those who know them really well will get to notice the differences. Their hybrid nature makes them all great little growers with a lot of speed, but their slightly shorter stature makes them good for both indoor and outdoor grows. The final size of your plants will depend greatly on the set up you use and the amount of space your plants have to grow roots, but plants can be kept even shorter by allowing them only a short vegetative period. A SOG set up is highly recommended for this type of plant. The breeders also recommend that growers give at least 6 weeks of vegetative growth with a medium to high light intensity for optimal results, but if you can't handle plants that are larger, you might have to make that time shorter. Flowering time is between 9 and 10 weeks for fully finished buds and if you grow with organic nutrients you'll receive a real treat in a gorgeous, healthy and great-smelling harvest!

Trip Seeds, Chile

Sativa-Dominant

Genetics: Destroyer x Deep Chunk/Uzbekistan

Potency: THC 16-20%

facebook.com/tripseeds

collectionseeds@gmail.com

The Afghan influence of this strain makes the high something of a creeper as it spends a good amount of time meandering through your body before it hits your head. The citrusy, floral smoke will finally settle itself into your mind and this strain's psychoactive traits will really take hold. If it all gets too much, calm yourself with a nice glass of Chilean red and a sobering chat about macroeconomics.

Dhaze

Spain's Vulkania Seeds are very popular in their native country, and rightly so. Even though they now work out of the Canary Islands, they're still much loved on the continent because Spanish growers know what's up, and they know especially well when a seed company does good work. Vulkania have always pulled out some great crosses of classic strains, and everyone loves those. Dhaze is a cross between Northern Lights (yep, that old chestnut) and a 2005 Haze plant, and was bred to maintain the most-loved traits of the Haze parent while being slightly easier to grow.

Unlike the Haze parent, Dhaze doesn't grow halfway to the moon and back. The Northern Lights influence helps to keep this plant to a medium height, especially when you put some effort into training in the vegetative stage. The breeders recommend only keeping this plant in the growth stage for a few days, as she will stretch in the flowering stage no matter what you do. One to two weeks of vegetative growth should be more than enough for your purposes, and an indoor grow set up, Low Stress Training and supercropping can be valuable tools for keeping your grow at a manageable height without compromising the final yield. This strain is ideal for ScROG cultivation and also for tying them down when the plants are still young. Your Dhaze crop will be amazingly uniform, with the plants only smelling slightly different at the end of the flowering stage.

Vulkania Seeds, Spain

Sativa-Dominant

Genetics: Northern Lights x Haze 2005

Potency: THC 19%

vulkaniaseeds.com

These plants love a lot of light and can also handle a good amount of nutrients, so watch their growth and use your instincts to tell you what to give them. They will be fully mature in 70 days, and should give a yield of around 400 grams per square yard of grow room. Three plants is enough to fill a square yard of space indoors, so you're looking at around 130 grams per plant in that type of set up; not too shabby at all!

Your Dhaze crop will smell like an Italian kitchen; the hints of garlic and onion (yes, honestly!) will give way to super sweet smells and aromas of licorice as well as the natural Haze spiciness. If you can avoid the need to feed when you smell this combination, you'll be well rewarded when the time comes to have your first smoke. The purple-white, super sticky buds give a gorgeous thick smoke and a Haze-y high that all sativa divas will love. The soaring head high will affect everyone in a slightly different way, of course, as Haze is a wild card and never plays by the rules. One thing is for certain though; this strain will definitely leave you feeling Dhazed and confused!

Diamond Valley OG

The USA's OG Genetics is a California-based medical collective specializing in strains that make the best of the OG and Kush lines. As these are probably the two most widely revered lines in North America at the moment, this makes these guys a popular choice for medical patients in that part of the world. On top of this, all their seeds are 100% organic, which should make for some very happy and very healthy patients in California! For this strain they've used a double dose of OG genetics, coming from Ghost OG and Skywalker OG parents. They then grew this plant through 5 generations to fully stabilize it before releasing it on the market, picking the best phenotypes along the way. That's the kind of breeding I like to see!

Named after the basin in the Nevada desert, Diamond Valley OG may carry OG genetics but it is definitely a sativa-dominant strain, as you'll see from its vigorous first growth and its killer head-body high. As the name might suggest, it enjoys a warmer climate, but this can be happily simulated in your grow room rather than outdoors if you prefer a stealthier grow inside. Though this plant won't get too big it will tend to branch heavily, so use your discretion in chopping off the lower growths if you wish. Diamond Valley OG nugs are especially dense when they are fully finished, so be sure to have absolutely stellar ventilation in your grow room; a tiny window open in your dorm room will simply not cut it with these bad boys. Good placement of fans and something to get rid of odors when you expel the air outside will be a necessity here if you don't want to lose any of your precious crop to mold or cops. Once you've made that mistake once, you won't make it again!

OG Genetics, USA

Sativa-Dominant

Genetics: Ghost OG x Skywalker OG

Potency: THC 22%

oggenetics.com

You can tell that OG Genetics are used to working with these kinds of strains, as they know how to preserve an indica stone even in a sativa-dominant plant. The Diamond Valley OG smoke is practically flavorless, though the hints of Skunk can wriggle through if you've got a particularly perceptive set of taste buds. The effects hit you like someone breaking an egg on your head; you feel it first right at the top, then the body buzz slowly oozes down to your shoulders, chest, torso and all the way down to your toes. However, after a little while this will settle into a nice balanced head buzz, too, and you'll be chatting away happily though you might be unable to move from where you sat. You will definitely sleep well when you've run out of things to say, too.

Diesel

Ah, Diesel; the quintessential sativa strain. If you've never smoked a Diesel strain in your life, you're missing out – and this Dinafem Seeds version would be a great place to start. One of my favorite Spanish seed companies, Dinafem have created their version of this legendary plant from a Mexican Sativa and an indica-dominant Afghani.

An especially great strain for outdoor gardens in warmer climates, Diesel can easily reach about 10 feet with a flowering period of 60 or 70 days, but despite its size and the sense of doom that such a monster plant creates, it's actually incredibly easy to grow. A little training might help you when it comes to harvest time, but essentially this lady is a low-maintenance girlfriend; funner, cooler and more naturally attractive than its more demanding counterparts.

My favorite thing about this Diesel strain is vaporizing it; it smells like a petrol bomb has just exploded some lemons and limes into the bag. Such a great taste is preserved by vaping, which will also bring the light, playful sativa high right to your head with no messing around. Such a high is great for all-day toking or a smoke outside a club when you want to keep dancing, and even rookie smokers will find it easy to handle. Get yourself a stash of this and you'll soon be a total convert.

Dinafem Seeds, Spain

Sativa-Dominant

Genetics: Mexican Sativa x Afghani

Potency: THC 12-16%

dinafem.org

Diesel Ryder

Canada's the Joint Doctor is known to most as the brains behind Lowryder, otherwise known as The Strain That Launched A Thousand Auto-Flowers. With such an influential plant under his belt you might think he'd kick back, relax, and smell the maturing buds, but no; ever seeking to move and improve, he's getting busy creating Lowryder crosses like this, a sativa/indica/ruderalis polyhybrid with all the traits of a Diesel plant that we know and love the most.

Counting the much-worked-on Lowryder #2, which is a Santa Maria sativa cross, and Soma's New York City Diesel as its parent strains, Diesel Ryder is perfect for growers who love the heady high and smokey tones of sativa plants but have a lot less than the 6+ feet of grow room they need to cultivate them. As with all Lowryder crosses, Diesel Ryder switches itself into flower at around 3 weeks from seed and finishes fully in 9 weeks, staying short in stature but big in attitude. Plants will produce one main cola and will stink to high hell at 7 weeks, so be sure to get some charcoal filters!

The resinous buds will be gorgeously shiny and when smoked will take you straight back to your best ever Diesel-fueled trip with its soaring high, fuel-like aftertaste and general feeling of all being well with the world. A great strain for any toker to enjoy!

PHOTOS BY DAVID STRANGE

High Bred Seeds by The Joint Doctor, Canada

Sativa/Ruderalis/
Indica Polyhybrid

Genetics: NYC Diesel x Lowryder #2

Potency: THC 17-19%

jointdoctordirect.com

lowryder.co.uk

Domina Haze

Spain's Kannabia Seeds are a fun and friendly crew who know a hell of a lot about cannabis and aren't afraid to show it. Though breeder Pato has one of the most amazing beards I've ever seen, the truly impressive thing about this young company is their ability to select fantastic genetics to breed from time and time again. Though they've got both Skunk and Diesel varieties in their grow rooms, it was this Haze cross that really caught my eye at the last Spannabis expo. A cross between a Black Domina plant, which comprises Northern Lights, Hash Plant, Afghani and Canadian Ortega genetics, and a Haze phenotype of Sensi's Jack Herer, Domina Haze brings together a plethora of great plants into one fantastic little strain that flowers relatively quickly and stays small enough to be available to many indoor growers. Guys, you've done it again!

The Jack Herer genetics within this strain means that your Domina Haze plant will grow long branches quite quickly, although it will only grow to around 3 feet indoors and will have well-spaced internodes that ensure even dispersion of buds in the flowering stage. Your plants will have dark, broad leaves and will maintain a good calyx-to-leaf ratio later on. The breeders recommend growing Domina Haze in a soil substrate with organic fertilizers for best results, and they say that this plant prefers an outdoor environment to an indoor one. It's perfect for ScrOG or Low Stress Training, and will respond to pruning by producing several top colas and branching out more. Indoors, you should keep it in the vegetative stage for 15 days only, flipping it into the flowering stage after that. Be sure to watch out for the plant's nutrient needs to bring out its best side in the flowering stage. The breeders also recommend trimming off any leaves that might hinder optimal light absorption as well as any spindly leaves or branches that aren't doing much with their lives. This will help get the fattest colas possible by the time harvest rolls around. The full flowering time for this strain is 60 to 65 days, by which time your plants should be bushy and fat and ripe for plucking! An indoor crop should yield 400 grams per square yard of grow space and one outdoor plant should give up to 500 grams.

Kannabia Seeds, Spain

Sativa-Dominant

Genetics: Jack Herer (Haze pheno) x Black Domina F1

Potency: THC 15-18%

kannabia.es

Your first taste of Domina Haze buds will have you salivating; the nugs smell of eucalyptus, spices and those aromatic candles that smell so amazing. The taste is equally spicy, but while you're thinking about how delicious the smoke is the high will sneak up, grab your brain and fly away with it, giving you a clean, confident, psychoactive high that lets you down gently at the end. Perfect for a nighttime smoke!

Dominator
(Kushage x Jack Herer)

Holland's Karma Genetics have already got some fantastic Jack Herer crosses under their belt, not least the well-known Jack O Nesia strain that crossed Jack with the fantastic Amnesia strain. Their work with the strain named after the late cannabis activist isn't through though; far from it! To create the Dominator (which should actually have been Sir Jack's nickname), they've taken the indica-dominant Kushage from TH Seeds, which is a blend of S.A.G.E. and OG Kush genetics, and bred it with Jack Herer #22. It's as if they can't leave this great plant alone – and man am I glad they can't!

I think the Karma breeders must have called this strain Dominator because she will dominate any other plants within her immediate vicinity – and you, too, if you deign to get in its way. Thankfully, they don't mind being bent, trained, and tied by ropes to keep them down – some might say they're even masochistic. This is good news for growers, though, as it means that if you let your Dominator plants get out of hand you can still bring them back to where you want them to be. Indoor growers with space issues might benefit from flipping Dominator plants into flowering when they reach a height of about 1.5 feet; it's not unknown for this strain to triple its size between the start of flowering and the end, so letting them get beyond 2 feet before you flip will be "no bueno." This strain can handle high doses of nutrients fairly well and gives away clones like they're going out of fashion. You'll need good airflow going through your indoor grow space here, as this will ensure that the branches are strong enough to hold the buds and will also ensure that bud rot doesn't take hold. Towards the end of the 8 to 11 week flowering period your buds will look absolutely phenomenal; foxtailing is my favorite marijuana trait and these foxtail buds shimmer in the light!

After a curing period of about 2 weeks your Dominator nugs should also dominate your nostrils with a very fuel-like smell, sort of like when you're filling your car up and you catch a whiff of unleaded. This will make you feel like you shouldn't have any sort of open flame around the area, but don't worry; the only thing that will end up blown is your mind! The Haze-like taste will give way to a high that doesn't seem to hit you much at all, then hits you like Tie Domi back in the late 90s. That hit will last forever, so don't have too much or you really will be Dominated!

Karma Genetics, Holland

Sativa-Dominant

Genetics: Kushage #16 x Jack Herer #22

Potency: THC 15-17%

karmagenetics.com

Energy Haze

The Bulldog Seeds have a very long and distinguished career in the Netherlands where they first started a coffee shop on the old site of a sex shop. Now they have one of the most respected marijuana brands on the market and even their own hotel chain. They've got to be doing something right – and that something is fashioning great strains again and again. For their own Haze strain, Energy Haze, they took two genetic powerhouses and melded them together in a flurry of awesomeness that resulted in a plant that gives an amazing high and grows like a charm.

With the genetics of the indica-dominant Northern Lights strain in the mix, you can be sure that Energy Haze won't outgrow your grow room or necessitate any crazy training to keep it within your windows. An average height for these plants is 6 to 7 feet, although keeping the vegetative stage shorter can help to keep the size of Energy Haze down. Outdoor growers should be looking to chop this crop at the end of October, whereas indoor growers should expect to harvest at 10 weeks. All growers will get about 500 or 600 grams of bud per square yard of grow space, making this a great choice for heavy medicinal users or dispensaries. Both the Kali Mist and Northern Lights parent plants are known to be very resistant to mold and pests, even outdoors, so we can assume that some of this hardiness has moved over to its offspring; although you should not let yourself grow complacent in checking your plants for any signs of disease or mold on a regular basis. You should also note that both parent plants are known to have a high resin content, so when it comes time to harvest your Energy Haze buds you will want to get yourself some good gloves; contact highs can be very intense and not fun, so beware of harvesting with your bare hands! Be sure to give your finished buds a proper drying time and a good curing period; with such amazing genetics in this plant, it would be a shame to get impatient and ruin what promises to be an amazing stash.

The Bulldog Seeds, Holland

Sativa-Dominant

Genetics: Northern Lights x Kali Mist

Potency: THC 19%

bulldogseeds.nl

As you might expect from a strain so named, Energy Haze will have you bouncing around the room like Tigger on the funny pills and blabbering just as much. Though the Kali Mist mother is 90% sativa, the Northern Lights influence will bring a nice body effect to the proceedings and stop you being all up in the head completely. This energy will eventually mellow out into a nice chill space that will make you never want to get up – except to pack another bowl, that is.

Fairy Godmother
(aka Godfather)

Now, I remember seeing *Cinderella* numerous times when I was a little kid, and to my memory, the Fairy Godmother was usually a portly old woman with flimsy looking wings rather than a large nug of dank weed. However, I know that I'd rather have some South African pot looking over my shoulder on a daily basis than a middle-aged busybody who'll probably need a piggyback at some point down the line – especially if that pot was bred by Budwiser Seeds and the awesome crew over at weed.co.za. These guys are tirelessly working to get South African strains some recognition in the wider cannabis community, and they're making more headway every single day. This particular strain, which began as a project back in 2007, has a double dose of South African genetics, with Swazi and Nigerian 99 influence as well as genetics from a Serious Seeds AK-47.

Budwiser Seeds and Weed.co.za, South Africa

Sativa-Dominant

Genetics: (African Swazi x Nigerian99) x AK48

Potency: THC 19%

weed.co.za

As the laws in South Africa are quite strict, Fairy Godmother has been kept between just a few lucky smokers up to now. Those who've had the chance to grow it, who number even fewer than the smokers, will know that this is an outdoor strain through and through, although it is happy in both hot and cold climates. There is work in progress to formulate this as an indoor strain as well, and to do this the breeders have taken the height down from almost 13 feet to around 5 feet indoors. Given half a chance, though, Fairy Godmother will still fly right up there! The breeders have also taken the flowering time down from 13 weeks to 9 weeks, which is great news for all concerned. This strain can be grown in SOG, hydro and soil grows, although the breeders recommend ScrOG for this one. As a true South African strain she loves the sun, so lots of light will be necessary in any grow set up. She's resistant to pests, though red spider mites do pose a threat, and she's sensitive to pH lower than 5. You might think that mites will be causing spots on your leaves, but this is likely to be the acidity; keep a pH of between 6 and 6.8!

The super strong smoke of Fairy Godmother is a lingerer, much like its annoying namesake, and can stay around for 8 hours or longer. The relaxing but creative head high comes on almost immediately, so don't get carried away and have too much or you'll definitely have a monkey on your back—or a geriatric pixie on your shoulder.

Flo

You know how there are some people who will forever be cool in your mind no matter what they do in future? I'm talking Alice Cooper, Doc from Back To The Future; those kind of people? Well, Canada's DJ Short is definitely on that list, thanks to his creation of the infamous Blueberry strain that spawned a million Blue offspring. However, he's not a one-hit wonder; far from it. With DJ Short varieties like this, a backcrossed floral line that's been around since the mid-90s, the world will always be newly impressed by this breeder and the plants he creates.

Flo is a 60% sativa strain that matures like an indica, finishing in a very short 60 days. When growing outdoors, the buds should be ready for the snip around the third week of September, and the breeder recommends multi-harvesting this plant over a period of time to give it super producing powers. The purple spear-shaped buds will certainly leave you wanting more!

Despite sounding like a great aunt, this strain is anything but slow; the high is super youthful and full of motivation, and the taste is like some serious hash. Flo is pretty perfect for an action-packed day or a smoke just before a family meal that's destined to be stressful. At least you'll keep up with all the gossip!

DJ Short Seeds, Canada

Sativa-Dominant

Genetics: Floral Line F2 x Floral Line F2, F5,6

Potency: THC 19%

legendsseeds.com

greatcanadianseeds.com

Gold Rush

I've often wondered what would happen if someone discovered reams and reams of pure sativa landrace plants in a part of Holland, in a place no one had ever looked before. Would there be a Weed Rush just like the rush to the Yukon in 1896? I, for one, would be the first to buy a truck and get a-rushin – and so too, it seems, would the guys from Holland's Spliff Seeds. If there was a strain at all likely to set the Weed Rush wheels in motion, it would be this three-way cross between Polm Gold, Purple Power and an Afghani indica. Anyone who's been lucky enough to grow or smoke this knows that it's worth its weight in gold and could definitely set off a stampede to Europe!

A strain that's only really suited to outdoor growing, Gold Rush is at home most in the Northern Hemisphere out in the open where it can spread its sizable legs. As an 85% sativa strain this one is going to be pretty huge, and it can easily grow to 6 or 7 feet given the right amount of root space. Even in cold or mountainous regions this plant will grow well, and it is almost wholly resistant to mold and disease; you could rub a chicken pox-ridden child on a Gold Rush crop and it wouldn't even scratch once. Despite this, the strain is suited to intermediate or very experienced cultivators as the growth rate and style means that newbies might be somewhat overwhelmed. This is one of Spliff Seeds' fastest flowering varieties, and when planted outdoors she will quickly get sick of the boring vegetative stage and begin to flower in mid-July. Harvest should be around the beginning of September, and you can expect to get a pretty massive 540 grams per plant. Like panning for gold, it's not the quantity with these buds, it's the quality; even a small stash of Gold Rush will make you feel like a millionaire.

Spliff Seeds, Holland

Sativa-Dominant

Genetics: Polm Gold x Purple Power x Afghani

Potency: THC 15-17%

spliffseeds.nl

These exceptionally resinous buds will have you drooling from both corners of your mouth and wondering if you can trade them in for a new Ferrari SP1. Don't do it though; the worth of these buds won't depreciate over time and will win you friends instead of alienating people and making them want to key your car. I think they might call this strain Gold Rush because of the way the effects zoom straight into your head; or maybe because once you've had a little you'll scrabble around on the ground looking for any tiny bits that you dropped. A gorgeous blend of head and body highs, it'll leave you in no doubt: this is a 24-carat smoke.

Grape Stomper OG

Gage Green Genetics, based in the U.S., are a great company with lots of personality and some strains that harvest the best of America's marijuana varieties and showcase them to the world. For this strain they've crossed their own most popular strain, Grape Stomper, with the "Jo Pheno" of North America's favorite, OG Kush (as in "Dude, I've got this sick OG Kush…no seriously, it's so dope!"). The "Jo Pheno" was selected as it holds the finest traits of the New York OG Kush and when paired with Grape Stomper, it creates a great medical strain that regular tokers will love as well.

Though different phenotypes of Grape Stomper OG can differ, most lean towards the sativa dominance and the looser, longer bud structure makes this very apparent. Most phenotypes will have a flowering time of 8 to 9 weeks, and every single one of them has a fantastically high yield of top-quality bud.

Your super frosty Grape Stomper OG nugs will be very tempting as soon as they're chopped, but a proper curing process will help bring out the fantastic grape taste and the citrusy aroma – and you don't want to miss that. Once the ice melts on your buds and you inhale that first mouthful, you will see how this is such a great choice for medical users, although even recreational smokers will be left smiling like the Cheshire Cat.

Gage Green Genetics, USA

Sativa-Dominant

Genetics: Grape Stomper x OG Kush (Jo Pheno)

Potency: THC 20%

gagegreen.org

Hapa Haze

One of the reasons I love Hawaiian genetics is that they seem to put you straight back on island time; everything feels good, you're super excited for life and nothing can bring you down. I think Centennial Seeds must feel the same way, as they use some great Hawaiian breeding stock to create strains like Hapa Haze. A cross between their best Haze plant and the phenomenal looking Waipi'o Hapa that I featured in *Cannabis Sativa, Volume 1,* Hapa Haze takes everything I love about the islands and infuses it with a psychedelic tone.

As an almost pure sativa blend, you can expect these plants to grow big – and to keep on growing. Not only will the plants dwarf you and possibly even your house with their size, they produce colas that are so dense it would take an intrepid explorer with a sharp machete to get through them. Be sure to check for mold towards the end of the 80-day growing period so you don't lose any of those gorgeous nugs.

The effects of Hapa Haze are out of this world: very strong, very heady and very stimulating. The high puts your brain right on a plane, lands you in Maui, hands you a Mai Thai and shows you some hula moves. Be careful with those hips though; it's harder than it looks and the last thing you want to do is put your back out and look like an idiot.

Centennial Seeds, USA

Sativa-Dominant

Genetics: Haze x Waipi'o Hapa

Potency: THC 16%

centennialseeds.com

Heavenly Blue

Based in the U.S., Master Thai of Master Thai Organic Gardens is a phenomenal breeder who has a lifetime of fantastic work behind him as well as a seed collection dating back to 1974. His Heavenly Blue strain is a three-way cross between Tahoe Blue, Princess 88 and a Romulan straight from Romulan Joe's own personal seed stock. Having such a rare and elusive strain to work with, and such fantastic breeding skills too, meant that Heavenly Blue was always going to be…well, heavenly – and it certainly is.

Created in 1998 and only fully completed in 2006, Heavenly Blue grows up to 5 feet and is best suited to areas around 7200 feet above sea level. The breeder recommends using a ScrOG set up and using bat guano, especially Indonesian ones, as these give more of a grape flavor. The plant is very resistant to both mold and bugs, and should give 85 grams of quality bud indoors or 170 outdoors. Master Thai suggests harvesting no later than day 45 of flowering, as a plant left longer will give more of a couch-lock high that you may not want.

Master Thai Organic Gardens, USA

Sativa-Dominant

Genetics: Romulan Joe's Seed Romulan x Princess 88 x Tahoe Blue

Potency: THC 17%

masterthai.com

Heavenly Blue tastes exactly like a frozen Welch's Fruit Juice Bar. Exactly like it. The effects are also similar; excitement, hyperactivity, mild euphoria and a trippy feeling. This is candy for adults, and it really does feel like it's sent from Heaven.

Hula Buddha

America's SoHum Seeds know how to make me laugh; when I first heard of this strain I imagined a big, skin-head dude with a killer tan wearing those hula skirt things and doing the pretty dance moves, and boy did I chuckle. The laughter gives way to respect, though, when you realize that breeder Ringo has bred a Pineapple Thai with Buddha's Sister from Soma Seeds at their facility in Southern Humboldt and in doing so, has created a heavy sativa-dominant plant that has some fantastic traits.

The slight indica influence present in the Buddha's Sister parent doesn't do much to keep the height of this Buddha down; he's a big boy, and, just like you when you smoke him up, he just keeps getting higher and higher. Tying down and training will help you to keep these plants manageable, and the huge, dense flowers might necessitate staking towards the end of flowering. Though the sativa dominance is more than pronounced in the growth pattern, it's not so extreme in the flowering period, which sits at a conservative 10 weeks.

SoHum Seeds, USA

Sativa-Dominant

Genetics: Pineapple Thai x Buddha's Sister

Potency: THC 17.49%

sohumseeds.com

The beautifully sweet, fruity buds will be long and solid and will taste almost as good as they smell. Be prepared for a very "up" and creative high that's good to get you going in the morning and keep you going all day and even into the night!

Humboldt

Named after the Californian county that has been so long associated with great marijuana, this sativa-dominant strain from Europe's Ch9 Female Seeds combines genetics from a pure U.S. Humboldt indica and Ch9's own favorite Jack plant, Jack 33. This is a limited edition strain and one that indoor growers short on space are going to be big fans of.

This plant will pretty much grow anywhere, but it is best suited to indoor grows where its relatively short stature can be best appreciated. The breeders even recommend it for closet and homebox growing, which is great news for sativa lovers who don't have miles of fields behind their house! With 25 to 35 days in the vegetative stage, an indoor plant can yield up to 80 grams of bud, whereas if you have the opportunity, outdoor plants can yield around 300 grams.

Your finished Humboldt buds will be very sweet and give off hints of that distinctive Haze smell; floral with a touch of acidity. Once blazed, these nugs will taste of jasmine tea and black pepper, and will wind you up like one of those little toys with the key on the side and set you off screaming across the room. An intense uplifting and creative high that will turn any lazy Wednesday night into the most productive day you've had all week.

Ch9 Female Seeds, Europe

Sativa-Dominant

Genetics: Humboldt x Jack 33

Potency: THC 18%

ch9femaleseeds.com

Jack Plant

Spain's Advanced Seeds have clearly got an ambitious streak – which is great for us cannabis connoisseurs who love to see the industry push itself ever forward! Not content smoking the already great Jack Herer strain, Advanced Seeds have taken those genetics and made their own new-and-improved version of it. Their Jack Plant is a mostly-sativa strain with some indica thrown in there to bring down the flowering time and make the smoke even sweeter than it already is.

This plant would be a great choice for growers who have previously only had experience with indicas but are looking to move into the sativa arena; it doesn't take as long as many pure sativa strains but still delivers a kick-to-the-balls high that makes you sit up and take notice. Indoors it can be kept to around 3 feet, whereas outdoors it will grow to perhaps double that. You can expect to yield around 450 grams per square yard of grow space, which is a good ratio for a new sativa grower!

If you are more used to indica strains, then Jack Plant will convert you in about two seconds. These nugs give a soaring, active, psychedelic sativa high that's worlds away from the couch-lock feeling of an indica smoke. Such a great effect coupled with the beauty of the plant itself makes Jack Plant a strain that the original Jack would certainly be proud of.

Advanced Seeds, Spain

Sativa-Dominant

Genetics: Jack Herer

Potency: THC 16%

advancedseeds.com

Juan Herer

I laughed out loud when I first read about this strain, which was a bit embarrassing as I was at a funeral at the time, browsing the net on my smartphone (it was a really boring funeral). I couldn't help but imagine our most-loved Jack eating paella, drinking tequila and looking at Picasso paintings while smoking up a big fat blunt of Europe's finest. I'm sure the late Jack himself would appreciate the comedy of this name and feel proud that Spain's Pitt Bully Seeds are claiming the Hemperor as their own. The Spanish cannabis community is so strong these days that any Spanish version of a classic strain is bound to make me sit up and take notice, and this one is no different. Pitt Bully have taken the Jack Herer genetics and worked their magic with them to bring a great new take on this already fantastic strain.

The Jack line is already known for bringing together three of the most popular cannabis strains around; Haze, Northern Lights #5 and Skunk. This great mix means that the strain is a balance of indica and sativa genetics, with the sativa influence just edging forward as the dominant presence. This shows itself in the way Juan Herer grows, as it exhibits that much-famed hybrid vigor and can either be kept relatively small or allowed to grow like a teenage boy. Its average indoor height is around 3 or 4 feet but outdoors it can reach up to 10, so you should consider both grow options depending on your goal for your Juan Herer crop. Due to this plant's ability to grow big and grow fast, the breeders recommend flipping them into flowering sooner than you might with other plants, as this will stunt the growth somewhat and keep them at a manageable size for your indoor grow – 15 days in the vegetative stage would be a good amount. The flowering period is variable, sitting at either 60 days outside to anywhere up to 90 days indoors, depending on when you switched to 12/12. The breeders recommend that indoor growers finish their plants by giving them 15 hours of darkness and 9 hours of light to get the best from their crop. You should expect harvests of 450 grams per square yard indoors and a massive 1200 grams per square yard outdoors. Who knew that Juan could yield so much?

Pitt Bully Seeds, Spain

Sativa-Dominant

Genetics: Jack Herer

Potency: THC 16-22%

pittbully.com

Juan Herer brings on a high that's chilled and calm but has a brain – much like Jack himself! Though your first few puffs will make you feel a downer in the body, this will quickly dissipate, turning into a very active head high and soon you'll be writing the sequel to *The Emperor Wears No Clothes* – and this time, in Spanish!

Kabala

There are a hell of a lot of seed companies based in Spain these days, and Seeds of Life are a young, emerging company specializing in autoflowering, feminized seeds of some fantastic varieties. These guys are at the forefront of a wave of innovative companies using the newest technologies available to produce their seeds and ensure that they're the best quality; Seeds of Life are passionate about treating their plants with the upmost care to get the best quality product to you. Kabala – named after the Judaist school of thought that Madonna follows – is an auto-flowering cross between Big Low, which has ruderalis genetics, and the uber-famous AK-47, giving us a plant that's easy to grow and grows some explosive dope. Thankfully, though, you don't need to wear a red piece of string around your wrist to let everyone know you follow this type of Kabala – the red eyes will probably be enough!

As an F1 variety, Kabala has three phenotypic expressions. The first is a sativa-dominant type that can grow up to 3 or 4 feet easily and has that telltale Christmas tree shape. The second is more indica-dominant and therefore a little smaller and fatter, and the third is ruderalis-dominant and will only grow to 2.5 feet in height. Thanks to the ruderalis genetics all phenotypes flower in under 20 days from seed and will be fully finished in 60 days. It won't be clear which phenotype you've landed with until quite far into the vegetative stage, but this doesn't really matter – each one is fantastic in its own way and you'll love whichever one you end up with.

Seeds of Life, Spain

Sativa-Dominant

Genetics: Big Low x AK-47

Potency: THC 18%

seedsoflife.eu

basilbush.co.uk

These plants are practically perfect for indoor cultivation but can also be grown outside where they will be smaller and may need a little more time to finish, due to the shorter light exposure. As the taste of Kabala buds are so fantastic, you'll want to give your plants a good flush to remove any chemically residue if you've been using synthetic nutrients, and might even want to do a molasses flush to get the best from your crop. There's nothing worse than growing a great crop of this strain just to skimp out on the flush – it's worth the effort!

You'll know that your plants are ready for the chop when you can't see the buds for all the resin and your dog keeps licking the leaves then being very quiet for the next few hours....that cheeky hound! Once you smoke up your first bowl, though, you'll understand why he loves it: Intensely aromatic, these buds are as good looking as they are tasting, and deliver an all-over high that hits all the right buttons.

Kalichakra

Mandala Seeds are a Spanish company known for their work with landrace genetics from all over the world, and the fantastic strains that they create from these plants. Kalichakra was created from landrace genetics from the south of India and South East Asia, and, as a nod to her heritage, is named after the Indian goddess Kali, whose association with the weed-loving Shiva makes her a fan favorite amongst potheads.

Unlike typical sativas, especially those bred from landrace strains, Kalichakra grows well indoors and doesn't even need that much light; presumably because her namesake goddess is looking over her and helping her along. A good choice for newer cultivators, Kalichakra will give many clones and enjoys hydroponic grow set ups, blossoming into a heavy-yielding strain under the right circumstances. The breeders recommend the ScrOG technique for growers wishing to get the best out of this strain, and all growers will appreciate the lack of odor at the end of the flowering stage. Kalichakra buds will be shaped like spears and your finished plants shouldn't be taller than 3 feet; perfect for stealth grows!

Mandala Seeds, Spain

Sativa-Dominant

Genetics: Landrace South Indian x Landrace South East Asian

Potency: THC 17-19%

mandalaseeds.com

These buds taste like After Eight chocolates, and the high is just as smooth. Without any hint of anxiety, the smoke sets you down on a cloudy pillow and carries you through the beautiful experience.

Kali Mist

Ah, the strain that gave rise to a thousand female pothead profiles on Facebook. There is no strain more popular for women to name themselves after than Kali Mist, for obvious reasons. I wouldn't be surprised if they're also huge fans of Serious Seeds, too, as I am. Breeder Simon might be one of the most interesting men on the face of the planet, and his story reads like a great novel full of surprising tales of adventure. Kali Mist is not the only Serious Seeds strain that's shaken the cannabis community in the recent past; in fact, these guys are so used to rocking the boat that we might have to rename them Tsunami. AK-47 and Chronic are already household names, as is Kali Mist, but Kali is the only one that comprises Cambodian, Colombian, Mexican and African genetics. That's the killer!

Kali Mist is a 90% sativa plant that grows in such a classically sativa manner that even the cops would have to be impressed just before they tore down your crop pointlessly. Though the original strain was already great, it was improved in 2000 to make it a bigger yielder and one that was slightly easier to harvest. It can be grown indoors, outdoors, or even in a greenhouse grow – and I've seen Kali Mists going beautifully in greenhouse grows especially. It also gives clones like any generous mother gives love. The average time it takes for a Kali Mist clone to take root fully in the new medium is from 2 to 3 weeks, and in my experience they are so desperate to grow that they'll grab whatever substrate you give them and refuse to let go!

Serious Seeds, Holland

Sativa-Dominant

Genetics: Landrace Cambodian, Colombian, Mexican and African

Potency: THC 17-20%

seriousseeds.com

Outdoors this plant can grow very, very tall, especially if planted early in the season. Expect a harvest date of around the end of November, whereas indoor growers should expect a flowering period of 70 to 90 days. By this time, your plants will be so loaded with flowers that you might not even be able to see the stalk; it will just be a massive cloud of bud hovering just over the floor. That cloud should yield about 500 grams per square yard of grow room when you can finally bring yourself to harvest it, so don't spend too much time admiring; get to chopping!

Kali Mist buds smell spicy and slightly sweet (which is the vision I assume the lovely Kali Mists on Facebook are trying to go for, too) and apparently is a favorite strain of women thanks to its strong and long-lasting medicinal effects that can help stave off menstrual pain. I have to say I don't suffer from that affliction, so I just love it because it makes me completely fucking ripped.

Kilimanjaro

Spain's World of Seeds must have friends in high places, and that's not a pun about the name of this strain....or maybe it is. Regardless, they must know someone high up (damn! I did it again!) to get a hold of such rare and phenomenal genetics as these. A pure landrace sativa strain from Tanzania, Kilimanjaro is the result of generations of crossbreeding by the local population, who refer to the plant as "the elephant flattener" – which probably gives you some indication of its effect! The story goes that the Spanish breeders named this strain after the huge stratovolcano that can be seen from the place of the original crop, as well as for the effects that can be similar to those you get from climbing Kilimanjaro; dizziness, head rushes and confusion!

Much like the mountain region that bears its name, this strain is big. While it can be kept to 5 feet indoors, its average height outdoors is 9 feet and above – in fact, it can get so tall that you might assume that its peak is snowcapped! Don't worry though, as this strain has a high resistance to mold and fungus, due to living in a wet climate, so even if it's snowy on top it will still survive. It will branch quite well and takes well to a green house grow op, and it can survive in even the most adverse situations. Indoors your yield will be about 350 grams while an outdoor plant will give you 500-600 grams of premium pot. It should be allowed to vegetative for 4 weeks indoor, or 6 weeks outdoors, and the flowering time sits around 70 days. Grab some friends for the harvest because it will be a trek!

World of Seeds, Spain

Pure Sativa

Genetics: Kenyan / Tanzanian Landrace Sativa

Potency: THC 17.7%

worldofseeds.eu

hemppassion.com

Your finished buds will smell of citrus fruits and spice, and the taste will be just as delicious. I first smoked Kilimanjaro while I was on safari in Tanzania; after a particularly tricky encounter with a mama lion I was calming my nerves with a beer when a local guide sat down next to me and started chatting about his love of Seinfeld. When he passed over the huge blunt he was smoking I was silenced for a few seconds while being repeatedly smacked in the face by the intense initial effects, then my mouth starting running a marathon for the next hour; I talked about Elaine, Kramer, Costanza and the social allegorical subtext of the famous line "these pretzels are making me thirsty" before trying to start my own African Festivus with a Festivus giraffe instead of a Festivus pole. They're lovely people, the Tanzanians, and that guide waited until I had exhausted myself, smiled at me then gave me another toke with an extra sparkly gleam in his eye. They don't call it the elephant flattener for nothin'.

King Kong

King Kong, a relatively new strain from Holland's ASG Seeds, has a lot to live up to; you don't name a strain after the world's most famous gorilla unless it packs a serious punch. Thankfully, this plant has the goods to back up its name, as it comes from a Northern Lights #5 Haze strain and a fantastic African plant known as Red Congolese – a combination that no one would want to mess around with!

ASG's Red Congolese cut came straight from Reeferman's gift of those genetics to the Dampkring head shop in Amsterdam, and after a year or so in their grow room the breeders finally matched it with an Northern Lights #5 Haze to create a strain for the biggest sativa divas amongst us. This strain instantly garnered recognition, as you would expect, and when you find it in your grow room you won't be disappointed. It usually finishes up at about 5 feet, and can yield around 450 grams per square yard of grow space. With quite a bit of indica influence in its lineage, it will finish in 70 to 80 days, which is definitely a manageable time frame for most sativa growers!

ASG Seeds, Holland

Sativa-Dominant

Genetics: Northern Lights #5 Haze x Red Congolese

Potency: THC 17%

asgseeds.com

With scents of pine and licorice, these nugs will blow you away – as will the mega-strong high. It's very uplifting, so go with it, but try not to end up on top of the Empire State Building. No one likes a show-off.

Krakatoa

In terms of impact, naming your strain Krakatoa is much like calling it the A-Bomb. A wholly volcanic island in Indonesia, Krakatoa erupted last in 1883, killing 40,000 people with a nuclear yield that was 13,000 times that of the bomb that fell on Hiroshima. That's some explosion. In taking that name, then, Europe's The Blazing Pistileros crew are telling you in no uncertain terms that their cross between Fruit Loop Haze and their great strain Mau-Mau will knock your head off; and if it's anything like the volcano, people might hear you getting high 3,000 miles away, too!

This strain is as tropical as the island that bears its name, with a sativa-style growth pattern and a fruity, mango-y smoke. However, the breeders at The Blazing Pistileros have kept the flowering period down to 9 weeks, and have tamed the plant's stretch enough to make it suitable for a SOG set up. The yield may be average, but the harvested buds will be anything but.

You'll want to schedule in a long curing period to get the amazing fruit taste of this strain to come fully out. You'll also want to tie down any valuable objects in your house and shut the dogs away in the bathroom before you light up your first Krakatoa nugs; this smoke is so explosive that who knows what damage could occur?

The Blazing Pistileros, grown by Jeffman

Sativa-Dominant

Genetics: Fruit Loop Haze x Mau-Mau

Potency: THC 18%

irievibeseeds.com

Krane Damage

Some of the newer American breeders currently coming up in the cannabis community are truly impressive – and not just because of their cool names and baggy pants. The MMB&J crew, and specifically the breeder of this strain and the guy it's named after, Krane Futures, are going to be making more and more of a splash in the community in the next few years, precisely because of strains like this. A sativa-dominant cross of DJ Short's F-13 and the fantastic The Black from B.C. Bud Depot, this strain began life an as accident when The Black turned hermaphrodite and bred out of the blue with the F-13. Normally growers are a little peeved when their plants decide to take things into their own hands, but on this occasion, you can be sure that Krane Futures was more than happy!

Currently, this strain is super rare, having only produced two seeds which were grown out by the collective. This means that if you're in the Michigan area and hear of some Krane Damage you better get yourself a stash before it's all gone. If you're also lucky enough to get hold of any seeds in the future, grab them with both hands and get to work! Krane Damage performs best in an indoor environment where it will grow to an average of 5 feet. She likes being in a ScrOG set up but will work best in a hydro grow op, though she's very easy to grow so will enjoy almost any set up you have. She's a super-light drinker and feeder (and probably a cheap date) and avoids getting extensively leggy and hogging all your grow room. After 4 weeks of vegetative growth she'll be at her maximum height and when forced into flowering will begin to exhibit a palette of colors that would make Picasso weep. Extremely thin branches will struggle under the weight of the thick buds, so staking will be necessary and by the end of the 10 weeks you might even have to be sat under the plant holding the branches up yourself!

MMB&J, breeder Krane Future, USA
Sativa-Dominant
Genetics: F-13 x The Black
Potency: THC 19%
medicalmarijuana-bottles.com

These purple, pink and blue buds will smell like Sambuca (or licorice, for those who've never experienced the nightmare of drinking Sambuca) and flowers (which are much nicer) with just a hint of spice. Once rolled up and lit, the Krane Damage smoke will dance around the room pleasantly, wait 'til you're distracted then smack you in the face with an "up" high that has no ceiling and will have you running through your daily to-do list faster than you ever thought possible. A great wake 'n bake smoke for the chronically lazy and the endless procrastibators amongst us!

Lady Tremaine

Canada's Whish Seeds are one of my underdog favorites. I say underdog because they've not yet got the recognition they deserve, but if they keep making strains like this then people worldwide are going to notice. I'm convinced that these guys are on their way to the big time, and strains like Lady Tremaine will very much help them along their way. Lady T is a first generation Canadian, bred in the Great White North from a Strawberry Cough and a Cinderella 99 plant.

When she's not hunting for caribou and eating poutine, Lady Tremaine likes to grow in hydro or soil set ups but she absolutely hates ScrOG. She is 90% sativa, and therefore should only be allowed a short vegetative period, after which she'll only grow to about 5 feet. This shorty can't handle her drink, and overfeeding her will quickly lead to toxicity, so be sparse on the water and nutes! She'll take a full 60 days after forced flowering to finish, but will then give about 56 grams per plant for you to enjoy!

The Lady Tremaine smoke is a very euphoric, social high, with a relaxing body buzz but an alert head high. This strain is perfect for smoking just before going to a hockey match or quietly watching beavers build a dam for a few hours while drinking a Molson Canadian. You'll be drinking the beer, that is. Not the beavers. Dam that's fine smoke!

Whish Seeds, Canada

Sativa-Dominant

Genetics: Strawberry Cough x Cinderella 99

Potency: THC 17%

whish-seeds.com

Lemon Thai

Lemon Thai was first created by an old Dutch company known as Dutch Flowers, although the only trace of them these days is the coffeeshop in Amsterdam. I've heard of tourists having a strange time there, complaining of its "crazy" owner, but I've always had a great time smoking their unbelievable hash and enjoying a great coffee with the locals. Clearly, Gage Green Genetics love them too, as they've been lucky enough to receive some of their fantastic genetics from someone in Hawaii and out of respect for their amazing work, have put Lemon Thai back on the market.

These plants are sativa through and through, although they're best suited for indoor cultivation and their flowering time sits at a reasonable 63 days. Your Lemon Thai buds will be crystallic and dense, with that telltale smell of lemon pledge and a whiff of peppermint tea.

My first taste of Lemon Thai came from a tightly-packed Volcano bag, and I remember being astounded by the pure citrusy taste of the vapor and the phenomenally cerebral effect when it hit me about 2 seconds later. The high is so clear it feels like it's made of glass and doesn't carry even a hint of paranoia; I could have had cops following me and I'd never even have noticed. I'm so glad this strain has come back around!

Dutch Flowers, Holland, grown by Gage Green Genetics, USA

Sativa-Dominant

Genetics: Thailand Sativa x Hawaiian

Potency: THC 17%

dutch-flowers.nl

gagegreen.org

Lime Haze

Now, I'm one of those annoying people who will send back my rum and coke if it has a lemon slice in it instead of lime, so I almost jumped out of my seat with glee when I found out that the USA's Green Haven Genetics had created a strain with the taste of my favorite citrus fruit. The breeders have bred this marvel from a Skunk #1 plant and one from the Haze family, so the high promises to be every bit as good as the flavor, if not better!

A vigorous plant, Lime Haze enjoys high rates of nutrient feeding and lots and lots of light, although it is also very forgiving and can handle stress and less-than-perfect conditions most of the time. You can either top the plant or let it grow as it pleases, but either way, the breeder recommends regular de-leafing to ensure larger buds at the end of each branch.

The taste of Lime Haze nugs was every bit as perfect as I imagined, and the high is a slightly delayed, uniquely sativa effect that gives you more confidence than Brad Pitt on the red carpet. Now if I'm at a bar and some bartender gives me that awful piece of lemon with my Sailor Jerry's, I can save my anger and just spark up a joint of Lime Haze instead – which will hopefully stop me getting thrown out of so many bars.

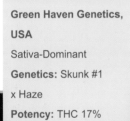

Green Haven Genetics, USA

Sativa-Dominant

Genetics: Skunk #1 x Haze

Potency: THC 17%

greenhavengenetics.com

Lucky Queen

Holland's No Mercy Supply really do take no prisoners when it comes to the breeding game. Their range of genetics is nothing short of incredible and they know it, bringing their best game again and again to the cannabis seed business. With crosses like this one, between a Sensi Seeds Silver Pearl and No Mercy Supply's own Santa Maria, they are telling the rest of the breeding community that they're here to stay and will continue to throw out amazing hybrids like they're dirty dishwater – which is good news for all of us who love their strains!

To create this strain, the breeders at No Mercy Supply crossed an inbred Silver Pearl-Santa Maria cross with a Santa Maria F3, making it an F1 hybrid. However, this F1 is of such high quality and is so stabilized that no further work is needed. The Santa Maria parent springs from the Brazilian Amazon, and as such is primarily an outdoor plant. Because of this, if you're growing indoors, the breeders strongly recommend that you chop Lucky Queen vertically, or it is likely to break under the weight of its own buds in the flowering stage. Of course, Lucky Queen can be grown outdoors too, where the wind can help her to have more stable branches. Even outside, however, Lucky Queen will probably need to be staked early on to avoid the risk of snapping stems. Neem oil can be a great choice for a way to fight any pesky pests that your Lucky Queen grow might have, although she's generally quite resistant to mold and mites. The flowering stage is a fun ride with this strain, as the plant grows paler and paler as it gets covered with frosty trichomes too. Lucky Queen gets so white, in fact, that you expect her to be listening to 90s hip-hop ironically, ordering expensive sandwiches and doing yoga. Just don't mention the 2007 movie Juno or Starbucks seasonal lattes around her or you'll never get away.

No Mercy Supply, Holland

Sativa-Dominant

Genetics: Silver Pearl x 85% Santa Maria

Genetics Level: F3

Potency: THC 18%

nomercysupply.nl

Your Lucky Queen harvest will be pretty heavy – heavy enough that you might be struggling to find places to keep your finished buds, in fact! Don't be afraid to pass some love on to your friends, as they'll be in love with you for doing so. Even after being fully dried, the buds will feel sticky, due to how much resin they produce – don't worry, this is normal. The buds have crazy awesome bag appeal but even better is the smoke! Energizing and stimulating, this high is perfect for going out to a party, going about your everyday business or boring strangers in coffeeshops by telling them why you drive a Prius.

Malva Loca

Spain's Dr. Canem and Company are a little enigmatic in that "treat 'em mean, keep 'em keen" kinda way. They may not be hitting the forums every day and giving sneak peeks of their latest projects, but I'm a big fan of theirs thanks to their fantastic strains and their love of bull terriers, an adorable breed of dog that I am a fan of. They clearly love their breeding stock as much as they love their pets, and have some seriously awesome varieties to breed from. It's no surprise that such awesome genetics give rise to plants like Malva Loca, which is a combination of Kali Mist and a fantastic variety called Nube Malva. To my knowledge, Nube Malva has in its family Estrella Malva and Nube Roja, both indica strains by Astur Jaya which have Lebanese, Pakistani and Afghani genetics and some South African sativa thrown in for good measure. The Kali Mist parent is the dominant one here, but such a rich heritage shows itself in a gorgeous smoke and a plant that grows like a dream.

With a 70% sativa influence, this strain is definitely one to be grown outdoors. It is fantastically easy to cultivate and will basically babysit itself with minimal interference from you; in fact, it's so forgiving that if it spots you trying to water it too often it will probably take the watering hose right out of your hand, sit you down on the grass and pat your head lovingly. Be sure to plant your Malva Locas in a covered place, as they're very easy to identify as marijuana plants – and also they're pretty shy around new people and might end up blushing, which they don't enjoy. When grown outdoors harvest usually occurs half way through September and will give you around 400 grams per plant. If you do choose to grow Malva Loca indoors, the flowering period will be about 8 weeks and you can expect an average yield of 350 grams. You should also note that indoors, these plants cannot tolerate temperatures below 64.5 degrees Fahrenheit, so make sure that your plants aren't left shivering; they'll remember it and withhold some precious bud when it comes to flowering time!

Dr. Canem and Company, Spain

Sativa-Dominant

Genetics: Kali Mist x Nube Malva

Potency: THC 14-18%

facebook.com/drcanem

In either location, just before harvest your buds will have absolutely gorgeous purple and pink shades, looking just like Scottish hills covered in heather. The plant, that is, not that slutty cheerleader you know. With awesome bag appeal, you'll have trouble keeping hold of your Malva Loca buds, as all the tokers you know will be enticed by their looks and beautiful curves (which, incidentally, is why they all like that cheerleader too). A great mild smoke with a soaring sativa effect.

Mango Haze

Holland's Rokerij Seeds are solely responsible for me doing absolutely nothing for an entire week a couple of months ago. One morning, I had the great idea of making some cannabutter with their Mango Haze strain and then making pancakes with it. I might have used a little too much butter, but the pancakes tasted so delicious that I did the same again the next morning – and the next morning, and the next, until seven days had gone by and I'd done absolutely nothing more than eat pancakes and watch pro wrestling in my underwear. Thankfully by the end of that week the cannabutter ran out and I had to go back to normal life; but even now, when I smoke up a Mango Haze bowl I get a compulsion to rent a WWE Universe DVD and take off my pants. You guys!

Those clever Dutch breeders created such an addictive strain by crossing together Northern Lights, Skunk and Haze plants, meaning that this might be an amazing strain to smoke but it is less than simple to grow. More experienced cultivators will welcome this plant into their grow rooms and will thoroughly enjoy seeing it grow beyond all the other plants in the crop and start taking up all the space in the early stages of flowering. With so much sativa influence in the genetics, Mango Haze will take a full 12 weeks to finish, and will yield an absolutely massive 700 grams per square yard of grow space. Of course, outdoor growers can expect even more, and deservedly so, as in the great wide open this strain will grow even more wild and leggy than its indoor counterparts. Stake early on to avoid problems with heavy buds!

Rokerij Seeds, Holland

Sativa-Dominant

Genetics: Northern Lights x Skunk x Haze

Potency: THC 17%

rokerijseeds.com

basilbush.co.uk

alibongo.co.uk

If you've ever had a Mango Lassi in an Indian restaurant and drank it much too quickly, then you're already familiar with both the taste and effects of Mango Haze. It's so delicious, so mouthwateringly fruity that it's almost impossible to stop smoking it (or eating it), even when your head starts to race and you can see you're getting to the bottom of the bowl. This might be the world's most antisocial strain, as it's so hard to just puff twice and pass. However, fight the temptation to splurge and just enjoy the stimulating, energizing high that hits you when the fruity flavor has disappeared. You'll feel inspired and creative as well as sociable, but beware that this creativity might end in you making Mango Haze cannabutter with your friends – and that will set you on a dangerous cycle, let me tell you. Thanks, Rokerij; your strain is almost too tasty.

Mantis F2

The UK's Trichome Jungle Seeds pretty much describe how every grower wants their grow room to be; a huge, sprawling jungle of trichomes popping up from the flowers and the fat leaves, skinny leaves and leaves who climb on rocks (retro reference, anyone?). With a promise to turn your grow room into a Jumanji of marijuana plants, they almost don't need to put out fantastic strains – but they do, like this Mantis F2 plant. A three way cross between Nap, Naze and the beautiful Santa Maria, this sativa-dominant strain really will turn your grow space into a jungle, with gorgeous results!

This strain is said to particularly enjoy a hydro system grow with a pH of around 6, or in a wholly organic medium. After 5 weeks in the flowering period your Mantis F2 buds will start to swell as if they've got either a problem with water retention or perhaps an addiction to Oreo Cakesters. Don't worry, though; neither is true. It's simply time for these buds to bulk up and start looking like they're ready to pop!

The trichome-covered crystallic buds will smell fruity and taste citrusy, with a subtle hint of hash along the way. The fast hitting high will creep down into your body as well as enveloping your head, giving a nicely balanced high for a few hours or more. Mantis F2 is a delightful smoke, and one that you can use every day!

PHOTOS BY OCANABIS

Trichome Jungle Seeds, UK, grown by Ocanabis, Canada

Sativa-Dominant

Genetics: Nap x Naze x Santa Maria

breedbay.co.uk

cannaseur.com

ocanabis.com

Mekong High

If you haven't heard of Dutch Passion, I can only assume you've spent the last 20 years cultivating your own personal garden in a cave outside Tehran, as they're one of the biggest seed companies out there and consistently produce strains that become instant classics in the coffeeshops of Amsterdam. Mekong High is a more interesting variety than most, as it comprises two different sets of landrace genetics, both received from the jungle; one from Vietnam and one from Laos, the often-mispronounced country just north of Thailand and Cambodia.

Mekong High is an ideal strain for indoor or greenhouse cultivation, where it can be kept to a manageable height compared to the six-foot size it will reach outdoors. It's resistant to mold and bud rot, and will be fully finished in 60 days. It will also have some great brown and purple coloration towards the end of flowering and the smell will take you right back to the 70s heydays of cannabis.

The high of Mekong High is just like a holiday to South East Asia; a total party vibe with very chill overtones and a hint of sunshine that makes everyone happy. Hopefully your night will end like a Bangkok evening too; on the back of someone random's moped with a ladyboy lounge's business card in your pocket, driving to get some more Sang Som.

PHOTOS BY GREEN BORN IDENTITY

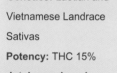

Dutch Passion, Holland

Sativa-Dominant

Genetics: Laotian and Vietnamese Landrace Sativas

Potency: THC 15%

dutch-passion.nl

Cannabis Sativa The Essential Guide to the World's Finest Marijuana Strains, Volume 2

MK Ultra x The Pure

I've said it once and I'll say it again; some of the best work in the cannabis breeding field at the moment is being done by private breeders with nothing more to gain than pushing forward a great hybrid and smoking some great weed. When you take money out of the equation, breeders tend to do what they do purely for the love of the plant, and private breeder JB of Spain is one of these people. In spring 2010 in the south of Spain, he decided to cross a male MK Ultra from TH Seeds with a female The Pure plant from the Flying Dutchmen, the latter of which is said to be an elite cut of the original Skunk #1. Its popularity would seem to corroborate that claim, as every grower I've ever met has raved about it, and the eyes of British tokers glaze over whenever it is mentioned. Quite impressive, it would seem – or is this an instance of mind control?

Given that TH Seeds' MK Ultra, which is a cross between the governmental strain G-13 and OG Kush, was named after a covert and highly illegal operation by the CIA that used mind control, torture and the secret administration of drugs to unknowing U.S. and Canadian test subjects, we could say that MK Ultra x The Pure is JB's attempt to surreptitiously make the whole world fall in love with Skunk #1 again; and if it is, then he's certainly succeeded! This cross brings out the best of Skunk #1's effects while enhancing the influence of the OG Kush

JB Genetics, Spain

Sativa-Dominant

Genetics: MK Ultra x The Pure

Potency: THC 15%

in the vegetative stage, making this an easy strain to cultivate both indoors and out. This hybrid loves warmer climates and lots of sun, and if you give her these, she'll be putty in your hands. The breeder recommends watering twice a week with very sparse application of nutrients, if any at all. He also recommends this as a strain for growers in the Southern hemisphere and Europe, and for everyone from beginners to the most experienced of cannabis cultivators. An indoor MK Ultra x The Pure grow will produce 50 grams per square foot of grow room.

Don't be afraid; the effects of this strain are 100% different to the effects of the CIA operation it's named after. Rather than feeling used, abused and wholly confused, this MK Ultra cross will leave you feeling alert, euphoric, and...ok, maybe a little confused. The fruity, Skunky smelling buds will bring you a very concentrated, focused high with that lovely fluffiness around the edges that feels like a virtual cuddle – or am I just saying that as a form of mind control? I guess you'll never know until you try it...(insert evil laugh here).

Moroccan Landrace

There are many good things about Morocco; their amazing tagines, their beautiful landscape, and the fact that you can go to the actual Casablanca and annoy whoever you're travelling with by saying "Here's looking at you, kid" repeatedly. However their fantastic cannabis plants have often been overlooked, and it's only now, thanks to Russia's passionate landrace strain collectors known as Gibridov (formerly Original Seeds), that this pure sativa variety is getting some spotlight.

Straight from Ketama Valley, this strain is incredibly, wonderfully unchanged from its native growth patterns. As a pure sativa it will grow beyond your expectations (and perhaps beyond your grow space, too) but it will also be very hardy and is able to look after itself for several days without water. For such huge plants they're also strong, although you might want to give some additional support towards the end of the 10 weeks they'll need to fully mature.

I am almost at a loss of words to describe this high. It's a euphoric, mind-bending smoke that surpasses your body entirely and sets up camp in your mind. It leaves you feeling like a whole new person, a good person, a person who can do things and be someone and might even be President one day; it's a smoke that makes you feel so, so good.

Gibridov.net, Russia

Pure Sativa

Genetics: Landrace Moroccan Sativa

Potency: THC 14%

gibridov.net

Mother's Finest

Sensi Seeds almost need no introduction. I don't know what corner of the world you've been living in if you've never heard of them, but please send your answer on a post-card as I'd love to go there on a "get away from the world" holiday some time. Even my Mom knows who Sensi Seeds are and the most extreme thing she's ever smoked was a cherry shisha on holiday in Cairo ten years ago – which gave her so much of a head rush she had to lie down. The kings of the cannabis seed industry have been making new strains for over 2 decades now, and in the early 2000s released a strain that makes me think their Moms are more hardcore than mine, as they named it Mother's Finest. A cross between the fantastic Jack Herer and a surprise Haze plant, this strain is a hit with any sativa divas and especially fans of Skunk varieties!

Mother's Finest is an outdoor plant that best enjoys summers with lots of light and lots of heat, so is most ideally suited to warmer countries. There's no telling what might happen if you put her in a cold climate with no proper coat or gloves; we all know that mother's vengeance is the worst kind of vengeance! To avoid this, plant whichever pheno-type you get in a good quality soil in a hotter climate and watch your plants grow so fast you'd think they were trying to escape; these plants can get enormous if they really want to. As a more Haze-influenced plant than many Jack Herer crosses, the growth pattern will be tall and sprawling, so be sure to plant tactically; only allowing a few weeks of vegetative will keep the plants smaller and more easy to manage. This strain is certainly one that demands a degree of growing experience to fully see it through, so newbies might do better to choose another plant for their first few tries. You will be thrilled to see your buds grow fatter and fatter towards the end of the flowering stage, which, depending on the phenotype, can sit anywhere between 8 weeks and 12; judge your finishing time on the growth of the plant and the darkness of the pistils.

Sensi Seeds, Holland

Sativa-Dominant

Genetics: Jack Herer x Unknown Haze

Potency: THC 19%

sensiseeds.com

With a yield of up to 120 grams per plant, harvesting Mother's Finest isn't going to be easy, but it is going to be fun. The Haze aroma will leave you in no doubt that your high is going to be fantastic, but once it hits you it will exceed all of your expectations. The giggly, euphoric, long-lasting effect tickles the inside of your whole body and en-sures a good few hours of joy. It's hard to imagine, but even your Mama would love this—and your Grandmother too!

Ms. Universe

America's Dynasty Seeds are a great company who've been going since the late 90s, and are going from strength to strength with every passing year. They've been growing their seeds all organically for over ten years, a move that pre-dates the current organic boom and proves, I think, that the company and especially main

Dynasty Seeds, USA

Sativa-Dominant

Genetics: Dess*Tar x Space Queen F3

Potency: THC 20%

dynastyseeds.com

breeder Professor P really does have the best interests of their customers at heart. These guys are passionate medical breeders who use Mendelian science to perfect their plants, and such amazing strains as Ms. Universe are a testament to their dedication. This plant counts some stellar varieties as its parents; a Kali Mist and Starship cross known as Dess*Tar was the sativa-dominant mother, while Space Queen F3 male had the honor of being father.

This plant expresses several phenotypes. The first has a Christmas tree structure with a 9 week flowering period, a little stretch and tight internodal spacing. The second is the sweetest one, with a little more stretch but more indica influence and a pink tone to the buds. The third, and the breeder's favorite, is larger and takes longer to finish than the others but foxtails like a beauty and taste likes a fruit salad. The fourth is identical to number one, except with a Hazey scent. Both the first and fourth phenos are perfect for stealth grows, but with a very thick structure and a high resistance to pests and diseases coming from the Dess*Tar mother, each one is a joy to grow and can survive newbie errors without much hassle. You can expect a yield of around 550 grams per square yard of grow room, and your stash will be covered in greasy resin and sparkling to the eye.

Like its namesake, this strain is a total knockout; just one hit and you're seeing stars. The berry, vanilla and Hazey flavors combine to make a perfect dish for your tastebuds, and then the psychedelic high kicks in and you'll be head over heels in love in about 3 seconds flat – and feeling a tingle all the way through your body that you haven't felt since you first saw Jessica Rabbit, had a hot flush and wondered what that stirring was in your groin area. I'm not joking when I say serious boners may occur when smoking this strain.

Nebula

Holland's Paradise Seeds have been growing pot since the early 80s. They have slowly but surely amassed one of the most impressive collections of breeding stock in the cannabis seed breeding world. When you consider that these parent plants have been stabilized over the course of three decades of breeding it takes on more and more weight; thirty years of breeding stock is nothing to sniff at! Though it's a secret exactly which blend of genetics comes together to make this Nebula strain, we can be sure that the resulting plant is a great sativa-dominant variety which was first bred in 1996 and is also known as Starcloud.

Despite the heavy sativa dominance, Nebula plants can be happily grown indoors as well as out. This is due to the very open structure of the plants, which facilitates easy training and tying if necessary. A SOG set up may be the most optimum choice for indoor growers as this will maximize the plant's production ability as well as making the best use of the space available – just make sure you know what you're doing before you do it! If you can fit 20 plants per square yard of grow room in a SOG set up, the breeders reckon you can harvest over a pound of premium pot. Nebula does have a tendency to stretch given any small reason to, so keep the lights as close to your plants as possible without burning them; remember that if you place your hand on the plant and your hand feels too hot, then the lights are too close. Indoor growers can also choose to grow in hydro, coco or soil grows, and a soil grow with organic nutes can help keep the taste and smell of your final buds at their best. Topping the weakest Nebula plants in your crop can work very well and encourage them to catch up to their more vigorous counterparts. Outdoor growers in temperate climates will find much success with this plant, which demands a minimum of 9 weeks in the flowering stage. Be sure to plant at least 3 months ahead of the first expected cold snap in your area, just to be sure. Whatever your grow set up, you should be able to see huge fat buds that are covered in resin just before harvest; at this point you'll see why the breeders named this plant after the stars in the night sky.

Paradise Seeds, Holland
Sativa-Dominant
Potency: THC 15-18%
paradise-seeds.com

If you can bring yourself to chop down your starry plants, your choice will be much rewarded. The smoke of Nebula buds is extremely sweet and tastes like candied ginger with some other fruity tones in there, too. The super head high will take you straight out into space and leave your consciousness kicking around in zero gravity, not really willing to come back anytime soon.

Nexus

Over the last few years I've had the opportunity to make more and more friends in the Spanish cannabis community and Eva Female Seeds are one of my favorite companies over there. Not only are they lovely people and very fun to be around, they're some of the most polite people I've ever met – and, my stoner friends, manners cost nothing! Their strains are also fantastic, and Nexus, bred from a Brazilian plant and a variety from the Blue family, is a particularly fantastic one for newbie growers that will still get you as high as a kite!

If you're looking to find plants for your first home grow, you could do a lot worse than getting a few Nexus seeds in. Easy to grow both outdoors and indoors, this plant only has two things it doesn't enjoy: high humidity levels and the SOG technique. Avoid both of these things and you are almost guaranteed to have a high-yielding and gorgeous plant that's totally finished in 64 days.

The resin will be almost pouring off your Nexus buds when it's time to harvest, like maple syrup off a stack of fresh pancakes. They'll smell like blueberries with an earthy aroma, and when you spark up, you'll be in a nice and relaxed but creative state that should see you being more productive than you ever thought possible!

Eva Female Seeds, Spain

Sativa-Dominant

Genetics: Brazilian x Blue

Potency: THC 16-17%

evaseeds.com

NY Purple Diesel

Oh, Canada. Sometimes, you make me want to move north of the border. When I'm reading about the Habs beating on a U.S. team in the Stanley Cup, or catching up on my weekly dose of Redemption Inc, or even eating substandard poutine, I start to get a craving for the home of Bryan Adams and Celine Dion. The one thing that gets me packing up my stuff to go, though, is when I'm toking on a true Canadian strain that blasts most other strains out of the water. The last time I finished my stash of Next Generation's NY Purple Diesel I even started up looking at house prices and dive bars in Vancouver, so good is this Canadian version of NYC Diesel. I'm almost afraid to get some again, in case I find myself drinking Canadian Club and watching the box set of Due South.

If you can save yourself from the lure of the Great White North, then NY Purple Diesel is a great choice for any grow room if you're a fan of the Diesel line – and isn't everyone? However this strain isn't just for indoor cultivators; outdoor growers will love the fact that they can show off their beautiful purple plants to the world. An outdoor NY Purple Diesel plant will almost seem to grow with every breath, such is the vigor of their type, and you'll be entranced watching them get so big so quickly. Indoor plants can benefit from being kept in a SOG set up that trains them to get the best out of them, although you will have to keep a sharp eye on these lest you end up in a Little Shop of Horrors situation with the crop growing right out of your house! A beautiful thing about this strain is that the plants get very purple very quickly, even without being exposed to colder temperatures. Towards the end of the 60 day flowering stage, which should end around October 15th outdoors, you'll be so proud of your violet buds that you'll beaming like a new dad – but your babies won't be covered in blood and other bodily grossness.

Next Generation Seed Company, Canada

Sativa-Dominant

Genetics: NYC Diesel

Potency: THC 16%

greenlifeseeds.com

A good, long curing period can benefit this strain, as it will help to bring out the already intense smells and flavors that the Diesel line is famous for. Your finished buds will smell like an oil spill, bringing environmental groups right to your door to help brush off the poor sea birds and fish. Don't be alarmed; just give them a toke on your NY Purple Diesel pipe, sit them down in front of a hockey game and chat endlessly with them about how good Canada is. Not only will they forget all about the Diesel incident, they'll get baked out of their faces too. They'll love it, eh?

Orgnkid's Banana OG Kush

Though I first read this name as Organ Kid's Banana OG Kush, please rest assured that this strain was created by a passionate organic grower rather than a child that goes around selling kidneys and lungs door-to-door.

First created from a Ghost Cut of an OG Kush plant, this phenotype was selected for its chunky Kush buds and smell of diesel and bananas. It flowers in 10 weeks and doesn't stretch too much, but really enjoys hydro systems and heavy, heavy feedings. It can also be trained easily into a ScROG set up.

It's actually unbelievable how much this strain tastes like bananas. This strain turns me into my 2 year old nephew, who's so obsessed with bananas you have to spell it out around him or he demands his 5th of the day and can't poop. Please, friends, if you get this, just let me have one bowl then pretend there's no more. We all know that I have problems with self control and I don't want to be on my 5th bowl unable to even get myself to the toilet properly without getting lost and confused on the way.

Orgnkid, grown by

Inkognyto, USA

Sativa-Dominant

Genetics: OG Kush

(Ghost Cut)

cannazon.net

Paka LoLo

I've often spoken of my love for a well-named plant, and at the risk of making myself seem like a Pineapple Express-style stoner who has nothing better to do than sit around laughing at the names of marijuana strains, I'm going to assert that once more: I love nothing better than a well-named strain. Paka LoLo, then, is practically made just for me; from the Hawaiian words for tobacco and crazy/stupid, this strain means crazy tobacco – and if that ain't the perfect description of cannabis sativa, then I don't know what is!

This dictionary-definition sativa strain comes from TreeTown Seeds, an American seed company who clearly know a good set of genetics when it leaps up and smacks them in the face. While wondering what exactly to do with the fantastic female of Barney's Farm's Sweet Tooth that was just kicking around their breeding facility, they tripped over their own version of Serious Seeds' AK-47 and knew that providence was smiling on them that day. The F1 cross was almost perfect, expressing a variety of interesting phenotypes that all had their own attractive traits. The average height of all of them is around 3.5 to 4 feet, so they can all be happily grown indoors, and the flowering time sits at 66 days. The breeders recommend that you place no more than 10 plants in a space of 16 square yards for the best results. All phenotypes are very easy to grow and can tolerate a whole range of nutrients, though some will grow much larger colas than the others. The breeders found that the best phenotypes flowered early, so keep an eye out for these plants and treat them like queens!

TreeTown Seeds, USA

Sativa-Dominant

Genetics: Sweet Tooth x AK-47

Potency: THC 15-17%

treetownseeds.com

harborsidehealth-center.com

All phenotypes display a good resistance to bugs and mold, although this shouldn't let you become complacent in ensuring grow room cleanliness. These guys grow best untopped, can be kept well in a SOG set up, and you should expect a harvest of around 350 grams per square yard of grow room from any phenotype. Be sure to note how silvery the leaves look before you chop them off – or use them for a tincture!

When breeding this strain, TreeTown were attempting to preserve the sweetness of the Sweet Tooth mother but increase the size of the plant and the amount of THC it held. Once you've finished your stash you'll agree that they've succeeded. The finished Paka LoLo buds will be as sweet as sugar cookies and tastier to boot, with a spicy flavor and smell, while the increased THC results in a hard-hitting and lingering high that will definitely let you know you've been smoking the crazy tobacco.

Panama

In Panama, the beautiful country where I recently spent some time smoking the local pot and getting blitzed out of my brain, weed is the rich man's drug more than cocaine is, so wrapping up a fat blunt of this strain from Spain's ACE Seeds and CannaBioGen should make you feel like a Rockefeller. This variety is a blend of red sativas from Panama and its neighbor Colombia, and will remind veteran smokers of the stuff Tom Forcade, founder of High Times, allegedly brought to the U.S. in the 70s.

Your Panama crop will be very uniform with strong structures and very vigorous growth. As a true sativa, it will grow to epic proportions if you let it, so it's recommended for outdoor growing only. You'll need some patience, too, to last out the 12 weeks before harvest, but trust me, it will be worth it.

Smoking Panama will whisk you right back to the summer of love; good vibes, good friends, and a feeling of pure innocence. Kick back with a bowl and a glass of sangria and don't worry about a thing. If only it would stick around forever!

ACE Seeds and CannaBioGen, Spain

Pure Sativa

Genetics: Panama '74 x Green Panama x Panama Red

Potency: THC 17%

aceseeds.org

cannabiogen.com

Pestilence

This strain, bred by Illuminati Seeds by Inkognyto, is interesting for many reasons. The first is its genetics; a combination of Abusive OG Kush and West Coast Dawg genes is always going to be exciting, and having such a great medical strain breeder behind the project injects even more intensity into it. The second reason to get so stoked is its awesome name; this might be the only strain ever to share its title with one of the Four Horsemen of the Apocalypse, and this name also hints at the strain's infectious qualities.

Like a real life pestilence, this strain kicks around for a while before it's ready to go, usually around 10 weeks or more. She will spread out as far as you'll let her, so read up on your training and staking techniques before you start growing this beauty. Pestilence will take over best in a ScrOG situation, but this Pestilence's stronghold will not be shaken, no matter where she's put. She's a high feeder and will devour anything you have to give and cover herself with frosting nugs as protection. Good news for you!

With a lemon and earth scent, Pestilence seems to be mild before she gets inside you, where she'll rip your head from your body and send it rolling around on the floor before you can pick it back up again. This is so enjoyable that it makes me think the apocalypse could be quite fun – though I don't want to know what War, Famine or Death taste like. They sound awful.

Illuminati Seeds by Inkognyto, USA

Sativa-Dominant

Genetics: Abusive OG Kush x West Coast Dawg

Potency: THC 18%

cannazon.net

Pineapple Sour Diesel x Maui Wowie

Some of my favorite strains come from personal breeders who may just have one or two plants in the works, but put their whole soul and being into making that plant the best they could ever hope for. This is true of Breeder C, who has been working on a Pineapple Sour Diesel and Maui Wowie cross for 3 or 4 years now, with fantastic results!

This mostly-sativa hybrid shows both types of growth; a more sativa, viney-type growth in the vegetative stage and a flowering style that's all indica. It can reach 7 or 8 feet tall and get about 3 feet wide, so many of the longer branches will need extra support to hold those thick, dense, indica-influenced buds.

The final nugs will be long, thick, solid and look as if they're covered in gingerbead crumbs, with hues of orange, gold and red. The taste is, of course, unmistakably sharp with a pineapple-y aftertaste and a heady high that is the frosting on the cake of this delicious strain. A cold beer and a bowl of this makes an utterly perfect evening.

Breeder C, USA

Sativa-Dominant

Genetics: Pineapple Sour Diesel x Maui Wowie

Potency: THC 18%

Pocono Red

Named after the Pocono Mountain region in northeastern Pennsylvania, this is a fantastic pure sativa strain from a very talented secret American grower, breeder and genetics preserver. A landrace from the mountains that give it its name, this strain is about thirty years old and has been beautifully preserved by this grower. Some Blue Cheese x Pocono Red seeds have appeared in the hands of select growers in Europe, but this strain is incredibly rare and I'm thrilled to be able to feature it here. The current holder of these genetics plans to maintain the line until it becomes well established outside of its home, then they hope to share these amazing genetics with the rest of the world; keep a sharp eye out!

As a pure landrace sativa strain, this is never going to be as easy to grow as your typical hybrid crop or even a heavy sativa-dominant strain. Growers with a good amount of experience, particularly with landrace strains, will fall in love with this plant and be able to nurture it through to its full potential. This really can only be grown outdoors, as it will grow to 15 feet and beyond – so unless you've got a grow room the size of a small cathedral or you are an expert plant trainer and staker, an outdoor grow is going to be your only option. However, if you do happen to live in Buckingham Palace or hang out in the Sultan of Brunei's personal grow room, you can grow this plant in both hydro and soil grows as well as Deep Water Culture. You can also grow in a SOG set up, in which case the breeder recommends flowering cuttings as soon as they are well rooted. If you prefer taller plants, vegetate for an additional 2 to 3 weeks. It takes 85 days for these plants to ripen after forced flowering, and you should look forward to nothing short of an enormous yield. The breeder recommends that you allow the root zone to dry between watering, so as not to overwater this strain, and also to flush during the last 10 days before harvest with ½ teaspoon of molasses per gallon of water.

Unknown East Coast Grower, USA
Pure Sativa
Genetics: Landrace Pocono Mountains Sativa
Potency: THC 20%

After such a long time growing, you'll no doubt be expecting big things from your Pocono Red stash. I suggest that you arrange your evening like this: get two very good friends over, but no more, and open that fine bottle of wine that you've been saving for a special occasion. Get your favorite, newly cleaned glass bong, and pack a bowl of Pocono Red. Breathe in deep, and enjoy the pure soaring sativa high with the taste of raw honey. It simply doesn't get much better than this.

Project GeeLove

I'm always happy to see the organic marijuana movement go from strength to strength, and in the last couple of years this seems to have been on overdrive. One of the foremost proponents of organic growing and organic seeds is Don't Panic Organix, headed by Californian breeder Eddie Funxta. This guy is getting so much respect in the community you'd think he was Michael Jordan back in the day – no one has a bad word to say about his work, and for good reason too. After creating his fantastic Diabolic Funxta, a true American sativa-dominant strain with Sour Diesel and OG Kush genetics, he's taken this plant and crossed it with the Dutch superstar Neville's Haze to create a project that everyone wants to be a part of!

This is most definitely a work in progress, and the breeder is currently working on exploiting his favorite genotypes to stabilize the most perfect GeeLove variety possible. The best genotype to date is a Diesel-like one with a high that lasts longer than a season of Cheers, although all expressions of this plant are phenomenal so far. As it stands, this plant can be grown either indoors or outdoors, although a Hazey cross will always favor the outdoor environment and will seem to grow every time it breathes in such a situation. Project GeeLove will take a fair ol' time to be properly finished, although the flowering time sits much shorter than the 24 weeks of its Diabolic Funxta parent – which is good news for those growers amongst us who have the attention span of a child of 6.

Don't Panic Organix, USA

Sativa-Dominant

Genetics: Diabolic Funxta x Neville's Haze

dontpanicorganix.com

They always say you shouldn't judge a book by its cover, and I say the same thing for this strain: don't judge a high by its hitter. Your Project GeeLove smoke will hit like an indica, reducing your body to a solid mass and possibly making you drool from both corners of your mouth. Don't worry though; that's just its way of letting you know who's in control, and after this first effect the high will crawl up the back of your neck and wrap itself around your brain, changing you into an Energizer Bunny of creativity and excitement. Much like The Thing, it will turn you from one person into another – but unlike The Thing, it won't take a scientifically-questionable blood test to see who's turned; you'll find them talking your ear off, painting, and cooking up a storm all at the same time, for about 5 hours straight. I was so hyped up after smoking this strain that I was afraid to go near cops, lest they think I was some sort of heavy drug user tweaking to a whole new level of madness. Who needs coffee when you've got Project GeeLove?

Pulsar

It's been a while since I've found myself in Spain, which is a tragedy for a couple of reasons. The first is that I often daydream about enjoying pintxos again in the Basque town of Mundaka, with a beer in hand and many old friends telling me stories, and the second is that the cannabis community in all of Spain has exploded in the last few years and is now producing some of the best contemporary strains there are. I've been a fan of Spain's Buddha Seeds for some years now, primarily because their strains are fantastic – and Pulsar is a great example of this. A cross between two fantastic sativas, one from the Netherlands and one from Central America, Pulsar is a sprawling, vast plant with a high that matches it. Such quality breeding stock has never shown itself to be so necessary, and this plant is one that I seek out whenever I can!

The first thing that anyone who wants to grow Pulsar should consider is space. This is not a small plant. Not only does it have extremely vigorous growth, but it is also massively expansive; think of one of those weird Japanese anime cartoons where something comes out of someone with a million tentacles and ends up covering the whole city. That's pretty much what a Pulsar grow space can end up looking like if you're not careful! If you're sure that you have adequate room for this plant, consider your growing experience, as this is definitely not an ideal plant for a novice grower. If you have the adequate space and the grow time under your belt, then you're one of the lucky ones, but you can still employ a couple of techniques to keep the crazy thing a little more tamed.

Buddha Seeds, Spain

Sativa-Dominant

Genetics: Netherland Sativa x Central American Sativa

Potency: THC 19%

buddhaseedbank.com

Indoor growers will want to prune the tips of the plant regularly, or, if possible, use the ScrOG technique. Outdoor growers should plant towards the end of the season, as this will naturally stunt Pulsar's phenomenal growth to a manageable level! Its natural flowering time lies at around 75 days, at which time it can usually be coaxed in from its huge growth with a promise of a cookie and some snacks.

Just as Pulsar isn't for rookie growers, it also isn't really for rookie smokers. The huge, spicy-smelling buds may look enticing, but the very strong sativa high can be a little too energizing for those who've only ever smoked a couple of bowls round the back of their school. A Pulsar smoke is super, super stimulating, so I love toking on this strain when I have to meet a deadline or when I feel like I'm about to fall asleep but promised someone I'd go dancing with them. Both situations usually end up with all of us laughing uncontrollably to the point of total laughter inebriation. A fantastic strain all round!

Purple Haze #1

I once played a game with some friends of mine that went like this: going round in a circle, you had to name a song that was named after a drug, and the better the song you could think of, the more points you got. There was no official scoring system and no winner, as we were really, really high when we were playing it, but my first song was Purple Haze by Jimi Hendrix and it was the highest scoring go of the game. Of course, everyone around me thought that the song was actually about Postronics Seeds' fantastic strain Purple Haze #1, which just goes to show the impressive influence of Positronics strains upon everyone of our generation. Jimi might not have been singing about this cross between Mexican, South Indian and Thai cannabis genetics that was created in the 70s, but he would definitely be a fan of it if he was around now.

He'd also probably be growing it if he was still around, as I heard that he was actually quite a green-fingered gardening fan. This is perfect for an outdoor grow for a cultivator with a lot of passion and some experience, as it will try its best to "touch the sky" with its hybrid vigor and might need some sativa-grower's knowledge to keep it with its feet on the ground. Just like its landrace family, Purple Haze #1 can become very tall and leggy, and will basically play by its own rules with regards to how it grows. It likes a lot of sunlight, as did its parents, and will work best with lots of room for root expansion. The flowering time of this strain is 70 days, meaning that it should be ready for harvest at the end of October outdoors in the Northern Hemisphere. These huge outdoor plants can yield up to 350 grams each, while growers who manage to convince this strain to grow indoors can expect 400 grams per square yard of grow space. In either situation, the finished buds will be so purple they're almost black – and are crying out to be enjoyed!

Positronics Seeds, Spain

Sativa-Dominant

Genetics: Mexican x South Indian x Thai

Potency: THC 22%

positronicseeds.com

Purple Haze #1 nugs are coated in crystals and have an aroma of freshly-cut grass and bonfires. Thankfully the taste is quite different – you'll instantly think of classic Thai strains and get excited about the high coming your way! Expect a creeping, encompassing head high that will lift you up and keep you on its shoulders for hours and hours before gently putting you to bed. And just in case you were wondering, Jimi's Purple Haze was actually about some LSD that used to come in purple capsules – although if he had smoked this strain, he'd definitely prefer this.

Purple Lemon Skunk

Hex Strains, a fairly new company based out of the U.S., won my heart when they named their strain in such an accessible manner. There's no messing about here; no being funny or trying to be clever. You already know that this strain is a mix of Grand Daddy Purple and Lemon Skunk genetics – all I need to tell you is that it was first introduced in 2009 and it smokes like a particularly awesome dream.

With a slightly dominant sativa influence, Purple Lemon Skunk isn't a skyscraper of a plant and so can be grown happily both outdoors and indoors, reaching between 5 and 10 feet in size depending on how you look after it. It is happy in both ScrOG and hydro systems, although your best bet will be a Deep Water Culture system with lots of space. If you top and trim the plant in the vegetative stage you'll be well rewarded, and the breeder recommends NPK ratios of 2-3-3 in the flowering stage. Your plants will attract fruit flies so be sure to combat that problem before you're swatting flies off your face and your grow room roof is crawling with them!

Hex Strains, USA

Sativa-Dominant

Genetics: Grand Daddy Purple x Lemon Skunk

facebook.com/HexStrains

Your Purple Lemon Skunk buds will be purple, obviously, with a floral, woody aroma that has a hint of citrus. The high will be just as colorful: euphoric, creative and uplifting; you'll be everyone's best friend, especially if you share your stash!

Purple Pine Haze

Based in the USA, SnowHigh is a fantastic medical genetics expert and preservationist who always has some interesting genetics up his sleeve from which to breed. I'm not sure how big his sleeves are, but he always seems to have something rare and interesting kicking around to create a fantastic new strain. For this one, he brought together a beautiful PineQueen Haze and a Purple Thai monster plant, bringing a double dose of great Thai genetics to an already impressive table.

Purple Pine Haze expresses several phenotypes at the time of writing, although each one is firmly up there in terms of height. With the leggy Haze structure pushing through to the fore, these plants can get a little out of hand unless you take some preventative measures; staking before you plant them is always a good choice. Most phenotypes will be finished outdoors by the end of October, although some may stretch for longer, in which case, patience will definitely be a virtue!

It's not often that I champion selfishness, but this strain is such a delight that I wholly recommend you keep it just for yourself or some very, very close friends. The tight, dense buds will explode into a fruity, energetic and dynamic smoke that has sativa written all over it. If you're not in a Haze by the first toke you will be by the fifth!

SnowHigh Seeds, USA

Sativa-Dominant

Genetics: PineQueen Haze x Purple Thai

PHOTOS BY SNOWCAP

Ray's Choice

No, this isn't the name of a male-driven sequel to Sophie's Choice starring Liam Neeson instead of Meryl Streep; it's yet another great cross from Holland's New Zealander expat breeders, Kiwiseeds. The story behind this strain's name is a lot less depressing than the 80s movie, too; in 1987, a friend of the Kiwiseeds breeders, named Ray, came back from a trip to California with a handful of cannabis seeds bigger than any beans that the Kiwiseeds crew had ever seen. These seeds were to be the starting point for the first indica plants grown in their part of the world; the game changed quite a bit that fine day.

Having grown out these magic beans and checked that no giant ogre lurked at the top of the plants (sorry, I couldn't resist), Kiwiseeds began to breed their own hybrids, mixing the Afghani indica genetics that Ray brought back with some stellar sativas that they already had. As a way to say thank you to the friend (and great breeder in his own right) that brought them back such great genetics, they let Ray pick his favorite of the F1 varieties. Ray's Choice was a 85% sativa plant that was a very strong grower, as if it was trying to prove that it was most certainly the pick of the crop!

Kiwiseeds, Holland

Sativa-Dominant

Genetics: Sativa x Afghani Landrace

Potency: THC 17%

kiwiseeds.com

dampkring.nl

Ray's Choice plants can be a great choice for almost all growers, as their maximum height sits at 5 feet making them suitable for both indoor and outdoor grows as well as green house set ups. It finishes fully in 70 days, and should yield up to 500 grams of weed for square yard of grow room. Although these plants won't grow too tall, they still show vigorous growth, especially when it comes to setting up some amazing looking main colas. The spear-shaped dense collections of bud will be so glorious to look at that you might find yourself in a Narcissus situation, except looking at your gorgeous buds rather than your own reflection. Try not to let yourself fall face first into your plants, as this might damage the branches and it will definitely damage your face when the resin covering the nugs attaches itself to your skin and gives you a mad contact high while you're clawing away at your own visage trying to rescue some of your good looks.

Once you've recovered from that, light up a bowl of these fruity, delicious buds and let yourself be taken away by the insanely "up" effect that shoots your mind out of a canon and lets it float back down to earth at its own pace. When all that's over, you'll certainly be thanking Ray!

Respect

I am a huge fan of Spain's Reggae Seeds. As soon as I start thinking of them, two things happen; I start singing Sister Nancy's "Only Woman DJ With Degree" in my head and my mouth starts watering. This is not because of Nancy – though she is awesome – but because I've smoked so many Reggae Seeds strains throughout my toking life and every single one of them has been nothing short of phenomenal. I get a little itchy waiting for new strains from them sometimes, but I know that it's worth the wait as they refuse to release a strain until it's perfect. I featured their Juanita La Lagrimosa strain in my first sativa strain guide, *Cannabis Sativa: The Essential Guide, Volume 1*, so it seems only fitting to feature that strain's offspring here. A cross between a female Juanita La Lagrimosa and a Cannalope male, Respect is so named because it demands so much of it – and because you'll get so much if you share your stash with your friends!

This plant currently expresses two phenotypes: one that leans towards a more indica style of growth and one that seems more sativa. The one with the stretch will obviously be more suited to outdoor growing, but both types can be happily grown indoors. Both phenotypes have a flowering time of 60 days, and both are easy enough to grow that even newbie growers will find them a pleasant challenge. Outdoor growers can expect to harvest at the end of September, with a huge harvest of over 2 pounds per plant, whereas indoor growers will be happy enough with 400 grams per square yard of grow room. One of my favorite things about this strain is the way the buds look throughout the flowering stage. Foxtailing buds look more beautiful to me than Megan Fox wearing an Audrey Hepburn mask, meaning that when I get near a Respect grow I have to be dragged away from my spot right by the reservoir, otherwise I'd sit there day and night watching those delicious nugs twist and turn around each other. I have had to be forcibly removed from one grow room before and I am not proud of it.

Reggae Seeds, Spain

Sativa-Dominant

Genetics: Juanita la Lagrimosa x Cannalope

reggaeseeds.com

I can hardly even bring myself to smoke up Respect buds when I am lucky enough to get them, but I never regret it when I do. They smell like wet wood and fresh fruit and other things that begin with the same letter, and the effects are pretty darn heavy. You'll end up feeling very sociable, very confident, and very desperate to listen to some Sister Nancy tunes while dancing around like they do in Kingston. Another great strain from a great company!

Royal Moby

I'm not sure if the Dutch royal family smoke cannabis or not (my guess would be yes, of course), but if they did, Royal Queen Seeds would be their official suppliers and the only seed company to have strains in the royal medical garden. It might be that the breeders over at Royal Queen are so dedicated to their monarch that all their strains are bred specifically for her; I just don't know. But if they are, I know that they will definitely get the royal seal of approval – this strain especially is a smoke fit for a queen.

As a mix of Haze and White Widow genetics, Royal Moby – which sounds like what Beatrix would call her pet whale – is a strong sativa-dominant variety bred from two of the best and most popular strains of the last thirty years. While the breeders were experimenting with some genetics, they came across a hybrid which retained the high of a pure sativa; this smoke was so huge that it was named Moby Dick and became Royal Queen Seeds' favorite strain – so much so that they made their own variety. I'm a particular fan of Haze strains and this is a hybrid that's really kept that Haze high in a great way. It also has kept the Haze growth patterns, and Royal Moby can reach 9 or 10 feet tall quite easily. Regardless of this, this is a strain that grows best indoors where it can be kept to around 5 or 6 feet with some simple training. Extensive branching means that Royal Moby can be a good choice for a SOG grows, although its very fast growth means you'll have to be

Royal Queen Seeds, Holland

Sativa-Dominant

Genetics: Haze x White Widow

Potency: THC 15-20%

royalqueenseeds.com

prepared to keep a close eye on it! After the relatively short 9- or 10-week flowering period, indoor growers can expect a very regal 60 grams per plant or 600 grams per square yard of grow space under a 600-watt light. Outdoor growers should be aware that this plant is a little demanding (like any monarch) and will need a lot of sunlight – its favorite outdoor grow location is a tropical one, where it will give up to 1,000 grams per plant. In any situation, it will require lots of top-quality feeding and should be watered often.

The bejeweled, massive Royal Queen buds will feel as valuable as the crown in your hands – but make sure you get over that feeling quickly and smoke them up as you'll be missing out on a phenomenally crazy, pure sativa psychoactive high if you don't! A huge, huge hit to the head, Royal Moby will have you so high you'll feel like royalty. It's probably why Beatrix likes it so much.

Shackzilla

I have never heard a bad word said about Holland's Sannie's Seeds, even in the competitive world of cannabis seed companies. This is probably because all of their strains are bred from specialized breeding stock and they make very strict selections from only their best plants. Such dedication not only speaks volumes about their intentions, it trickles down throughout the whole process and you can almost taste it in the smoke!

Shackzilla was created by breeding a Super Silver Haze with Sannie's own Shack strain, which is a blend of Sannie's Jack and a Shiva strain. The Sannie's breeders have been using Shack for numerous years now, and it's one of their favorite breeding strains for a reason: it has a very short flowering time and a growth pattern that's easy to control. Both of these traits come in handy when dealing with a sativa hybrid, and in Shackzilla they bring forth a flowering time that sits at 10 weeks as well as a shorter plant than you would expect from a Super Silver Haze cross. Shackzilla is best suited to an indoor grow, but one that has plenty of space and would facilitate some extensive training if that became necessary. If you have a grow space that will let this monster grow to its full potential, then you might as well start buying some kegs and securing all the fragile or expensive items in your house, because in 11 weeks time you're going to be having one hell of a Shackzilla-driven party in your house – and it's going to be a biggie. With a potential yield of up to 700 grams per square yard of grow space, you're going to have enough stash to share with the population of Monaco, so send the invites out right now. Your picture-perfect, shimmering buds are going to be the hottest ticket in town.

Sannie's Seeds, Holland
Sativa-Dominant
Genetics: Super Silver Haze x Shack F1
Potency: THC 23%
sanniesshop.com
opengrow.com

Here's how your Shackzilla party is going to pan out; there's going to be a bit of awkward conversation and a bit of a ruckus over what Damian Marley track is playing, and someone will make a slightly inappropriate joke that kinda kills the mood. Then you're going to start passing round that three-foot bong of yours and suddenly a sweet, Haze-y fog will settle over the room and engulf everyone's heads. Before you know it, strangers will be chatting like their lives depend on it and every single person in the room will have a giant grin plastered onto their faces. You might even find Derek from your math class and Jascinta from next door getting frisky in the bathroom, but it's not their fault; such is the explosive and long-lasting social lubricant power of the Shackzilla!

Shamanic Haze

Holland's De Sjamaan certainly knows how to market his strains. Even before I knew anything about this strain beyond the name, I was fascinated by it. The phrase "Shamanic Haze" conjures up images of exotic villagers all coming together in one vast collective effervescence, praying at the altar of weed and enjoying their time together while high as a cloud. The first time I heard someone talk about it I imagined rolling green hills misty in the morning dew, with stoners laying, spinning and running uphill and downhill in the grip of some mystical power. I wanted in.

The reality of the effects of Shamanic Haze might not be that far from my original vision. Having been in the game since 1998, De Sjamaan certainly knows how to create a crazy strain and he's earned his nickname through an almost magical mastery of cannabis genetics – and who knows, he might even be able to control the feelings of a village full of people, too. He has most definitely tapped into the best traits of the Haze line, with Shamanic Haze being a cross between a top quality Haze plant and an enigmatic strain known only as "X".

De Sjamaan, Holland

Sativa-Dominant

Genetics: 'X' x Haze

Potency: THC 19%

sjamaan.com

With such sativa influence in its gene pool, its not surprising that this strain grows almost as the epitome of that type. Like all sativas, it is happiest when it's allowed to be the tallest in the class, and will easily reach 6 feet without even breaking a sweat. It will also be as leggy as it is tall, although the slight indica presence will stop it from taking over your whole garden. If your grow space is restricted in any way, you might want to consider growing this plant in the ScROG method or training it in another way. Shamanic Haze is only recommended for indoor growing. By the time you reach the end of the flowering period, half your stems and branches should be covered with long, luscious flowers and they should look as if someone's just poured glitter glue all over them: sticky, shimmering and utterly delicious. All this should happen around the 75th day, and when you chop your centerfold-worthy tree down you can expect to weigh in around 100 grams of dank nugs per square yard of grow space.

I remember my hands shaking while I was trying to light up my first Shamanic Haze bowl, so nervous was I about what I was going to experience. Would I hang on to reality or be whisked away completely and irrevocably? I didn't quite end up rolling in the wet grass of a country morning praying to Jah, but I did feel that I'd stepped into a mysticism as yet untouched by myself. Did I really get there, or is this just the magic of De Sjamaan? We'll never know.

Shanti

I'm not sure if Holland's Ministry of Cannabis are an official governmental organization —you can never quite tell when it comes to the Netherlands — but they've definitely earned their stripes in the breeding game over the years. For years these guys have been popping out great strains, and this one, Shanti, takes its name from the Sanskrit word for inner peace. As the genetics come from two sativa plants, one pure and one hybrid, I have no doubt at all in believing that this strain will bring me inner peace — though that might only come through after 4 hours of bounding around like a maniac and being unable to form a proper conversation for longer than 30 seconds at a time. That's fine though; peace is peace, whenever it comes!

Shanti was first created in 2008 in the Netherlands, and is a 75% sativa-dominant variety suitable for growers of all experience, especially in Europe and North America. The breeders instantly recognized her as unique amongst their strains and so set to work stabilizing and perfecting her. Shanti will grow really well in both SOG and ScrOG set ups, where the training will maximize her potential. She likes to grow very branchy but she won't grow beyond 3 or 4 feet in height regardless of whether you grow indoors or outdoors. Hydro grows should be avoided, however, as Shanti is something of a young hippy and very much favors organic soil grows. The breeders recommend vegetating for 4 weeks in soil, and ensuring lots of good ventilation in the grow room to avoid mold as her resistance to it could use a little work.

Ministry of Cannabis, Holland

Sativa-Dominant

Genetics: Sativa x Sativa Hybrid

Potency: THC 15%

ministryofcannabis.com

The flowering time is 9 weeks, and the breeders recommend watering with reverse osmosis water in the final 2 weeks if possible. Your harvest will be a joy, as the high calyx-to-leaf ratio means that trimming is easy, and this will make a difference when you're trying to bring down 350 grams of great bud per outdoor plant!

Your finished Shanti buds will smell of a huge bunch of just-ripened flowers, which might cause trouble if your girlfriend gets home and thinks you've treated her for once, only to find out you're actually high as hell. You should be able to placate her by sharing your homegrown stash, as these buds deliver an extremely happy high that should negate any feelings of flower-based animosity. The light smoke seems to be going in your ears, eyes and nose all at once and massaging your brain from the inside of your skull. Once you both find the inner peace that Shanti promises you can order in a giant pizza and everything will be gravy.

Shoreline

The Devil's Harvest Seed Company are one of the newer crews on my radar. Based in the Netherlands, these two breeders are doing great work so far, and seem to be focusing on quality rather than quantity with their catalog, which gets them one gold star from me. They get another gold star for resurrecting one of Texas' most-famed and most-loved strains from years gone by. My great friend Rio, an Austin native and killer DJ, lit up when I even mentioned that I was going to put this strain in the book. And by that I mean his face lit up and also he had to smoke a bowl just to calm himself down.

Legend has it that Shoreline's daddy, the Sensi Skunk strain, made its way to the USA and was named for the Shoreline Amphitheater just after a Grateful Dead concert where it got most of the fans high as hell. A cross between an old Sensi Skunk and Oasis, which is a Dutch Passion Northern Lights #2 breed, Shoreline is some of the skunkiest shit that ever existed. Right from the get-go there's no dispute about Shoreline's heritage; even in the vegetative stage it grows just as you remember a Skunk strain to grow. The hybrid vigor is out in full force with very speedy growth and an 8-week finishing time, by which time the buds will be completely purple and so stinky you have to install a NASA-grade ventilation system in your grow room. Of course, this will be much easier to do at the start of the grow cycle, so get some heavy-duty charcoal filters in your grow space before you plant and remember that you don't want to attract any negative attention. Better safe than sorry!

Devil's Harvest Seed Company, Holland

Sativa-Dominant

Genetics: Sensi Skunk x Oasis

Potency: THC 18%

facebook.com/DevilsHarvestSeeds

thedevilsharvestseeds.com

Be aware that when you've harvested your Shoreline buds vacuum sealing them in baggies will be 100% necessary unless you want to be known as Skunk Boy in the local community. It's not often that you get a strain that tastes as strong as it smells, but when you take your first mouthful of Shoreline smoke you'll feel like you just popped a bud in your mouth and are sucking on it like a lollipop. Your mind will be on fire and your body will be made of Jell-O; this amazing strain is a couch-lock thinker, so get ready to enjoy the bizarre thoughts of your friends for some time, because you ain't getting up anytime soon. Rio and I chatted about Skrillex and the state of dubstep in general for about twelve hours straight and man, that was the best conversation EVER.

SmellyBerry

Ah, UGORG, you continue to steal my heart. Not only do you come from the UK, land of mushy peas, all good music and my grandma, but you consistently come out with great strains and you sell art on your website. If you were also 6 foot and a redhead I might be trying to arrange the world's first human-to-seed-company marriage (although I'm sure it wouldn't pass in Texas). As if all this wasn't cool enough, they've now come out with SmellyBerry, which is a cross of DJ Short's Blueberry with an elusive strain known as Blues – although we can probably guess what family line this strain comes from.

SmellyBerry is a strain that can be grown both indoors and outdoors, although outdoor cultivation will take a little more effort and experience on the part of the grower; picking the exact right time to plant this strain will make a big difference in the final yield and the plant's overall health. The influence of the mostly-indica Blueberry parent comes through very much in the growth patterns of this plant, which will stay a lot more short and squat than you might be used to with your sativa strains. This will also exhibit

Underground Originals, UK

Sativa-Dominant

Genetics: Blues x Blueberry

Potency: THC 17-19%

ugorg.com

good branching and numerous bud sites, although it's the growth of the buds themselves that will really leave you amazed. The buds quickly become large colas and cover themselves in thick, deep layers of resin that make them look far too valuable to be touched! As with all strains from the Blue line, SmellyBerry buds will turn purple and blue, and especially so when they're exposed to lower temperatures. Indoor growers should let this one linger in the vegetative stage for a little longer than usual, as this will greatly increase the final yield. Outdoor growers who've planted in the right part of the season will enjoy phenomenal yields of buds that have amazing bag appeal! Indoor flowering time is 7 to 8 weeks after forced flowering, and a good harvest time outdoors is the start of October.

SmellyBerry is a very relaxing smoke; with a taste of Blueberry pancakes and maple syrup and a calming head high that's all awake but very chill, you couldn't ask for a better mellow smoke. The effects will massage your body from the inside out, as if a million little smoke people are running up and down your muscles, and then open up your brain to whatever wants to get in. This is an especially good strain for medicinal patients who are suffering from stiff muscles and spasms, and it may help to kill pain in those with chronic pain. This is also a potentially good strain for those with mental health issues, and for the rest of us, it's simply an amazing treat.

Somaui

I don't know if I've mentioned, but I quite like Hawaiian strains. OK, so I do know that I've mentioned this, but in this particular case, we should disregard my immediate bias. No matter whether you're a sativa diva, the world's biggest fan of Akebono Taro (Google him) or an absolute hater of the fiftieth state, you are going to love this strain. Holland's celebrated Soma Seeds have harnessed the best of island genetics by crossing a Hawaiian landrace sativa strain with the fantastic G-13 Haze cross that everyone loves, to create a plant that's American through and through – but still has that tropical side that makes it so delicious.

Though this plant will entice all, it's definitely not recommended for new growers or those who don't have much time to dedicate to looking after their plants. It should most definitely be grown outdoors, unless you want to end up closed out of your own grow room by huge plants that take no prisoners. Keeping it to a reasonable size indoors is simply too difficult, but outdoors you might have more success in taming its growth; I've had several growers tell me that supercropping works brilliantly with this strain, but if you're a little too afraid to go down that route, then bending and tying stems early on can be a real help too. The Hawaiian landrace genetics mean that this plant enjoys a long flowering time, sitting at 12 to 14 weeks depending on the climate, but while newbie growers might have an emotional breakdown waiting all that time, experienced growers will enjoy this extra time the most as the thin buds will start to thicken up on the inside and begin to really look impressive. Towards the end of flowering the white buds will take on a pinkish hue and start to look truly tropical. The smell, too, will be of flowers and beachy days, and as the buds are very resistant to mold, these last couple of weeks should be a total breeze. Your harvest will be medium high, with great buds that are not only easy to manicure but dry like a dream. A great strain to grow for the more experienced cultivators!

Soma Seeds, Holland

Sativa-Dominant

Genetics: G-13 Haze x Hawaiian Sativa

Potency: THC 18%

somaseeds.nl

Your finished Somaui buds will be tinted with pink and smell like a bouquet of roses – in fact, if your girlfriend's birthday is coming up, I'm sure she'll appreciate a set of Somaui buds more than some dying roses from the gas station. Think about it; once she's done sniffing, she can get high as shit on the incredibly strong sativa smoke that turns your head into an ideas factory – although all these ideas will involve eating a lot of candy and watching reruns of "Seinfeld." Sounds like a good birthday to me!

Sour Lemon OG

The Emerald Triangle has to be one of the most popular seed companies with older American smokers, as they're all about preserving the best older stains from that part of the world and making them current once more; kind of like when your Grandpa tells you endless stories about some old guy who used to live in your town, Blind Steve, because he wants you to understand exactly what that dude was about. The difference here is that while you're playing Call Of Duty while your Grandpa jabbers on, we're all enthralled by Emerald Triangle's seemingly endless supply of quality old school genetics and can't wait to see what they come up with next. This Sour Lemon OG is a particularly phenomenal cross, as it can count OG Kush, Mexican sativa and Afghani plants in its family tree (if you'll pardon the pun) and is the favorite plant of many an old-time smoker.

To create this plant, a unique Lemony phenotype of OG Kush, everyone's favorite strain, was bred with a California Sour, which means that the hybrid is only just sativa-dominant. As such, a Sour Lemon OG crop will have a heavy structure, even though the sativa genetics dictate that it will grow tall and lanky, following a mad rush of growth in the vegetative stage. The plant displays a symphony of different green colorations and its pre-flowers will have a hint of yellow. Growers shouldn't panic when their crop looks to be stagnating somewhat in the first flush of flowering; this strain will explode into rapid flower growth after a couple of weeks in its final stage. Though the initially soft buds will make you think something is awry, they will quickly and quietly turn into big puffy colas, just like a weedy kid who hits puberty; all those burgers and chips suddenly catch up with them and make them balloon into Eric Cartman. These plants enjoy being trained, and make sure you keep an eye on its levels of nutrients, especially if you're growing in hydro. Outdoors growers can expect to harvest around late October in the Northern Hemisphere, while indoors growers can look to chop around the 74-day mark. Get some buddies round for the harvesting job as under the right conditions, this plant can yield some serious buddage.

Emerald Triangle Seeds, USA

Sativa-Dominant

Genetics: (Mexican Sativa x Afghani) x OG Kush (Lemon OG)

Potency: THC 15-17%

emeraldtriangle-seeds.co.uk

Your harvested Sour Lemon OG nugs will benefit endlessly from a long curing stage; the gorgeously sharp citrusy aroma will have your mouth watering before you know it. The slight Kush smell turns into a slight Kush effect with a very big mental splash, making this strain great for parties or for a wake 'n bake on busy days.

Sour OG

The Diesel line of marijuana has to be one of my absolute favorites. The amount of strains that use Sour Diesel as their parents increases almost every day, and each one is pretty amazing in its own way. This Sour OG from 420Clones.com is a cross between a fantastic Sour Diesel plant and a prized OG Kush pheno, making it a 60/40 sativa/indica beauty that's everything you could want from a pot plant. The Sour Diesel parent is a very sativa-dominant variety that comes from the famed ChemDawg line, whereas the OG Kush is probably the most well-known and well-loved variety in North America at the moment. Seriously – as soon as anyone hears you've got Kush, you're like the most popular kid in the playground and everyone suddenly wants you to come over for a smoke. Keep it on the down low that your Sour OG stash is a Kush family member, and you might just be able to hang on to it for yourself!

Those who want more from their pot than a Kush name tag will find lots to love in this strain. Its family tree includes such strains as Northern Lights, Skunk, Hawaiian and ChemDawg, so it's got more expectation on its shoulders than a new Jonas Brother (although it's a lot less irritating). You'll find that the Skunk heritage comes through in the smell, which will permeate your grow room towards the end of flowering. A skunk smell is always welcome but make sure your ventilation is sufficient!

420Clones.com, USA

Sativa-Dominant

Genetics: Sour Diesel x OG Kush

Potency: THC 17%

420clones.com

Sour OG plants can be grown both indoors and out-doors, but as they can get up to 6 feet, indoor growers will have to ensure that they have enough space for their plants to fill out if they want to get the best out of each grow. Sour OG plants can respond particularly well to top-ping, but make sure you know what you're doing before you go all choppy, get carried away and end up with a benign stump of a sad plant with no chance of growing. The solid structure of the plant means that it should be able to carry its own weight without any help from you, but be sure to check your grow room for any signs of drooping branches as the buds get bigger and bigger. At 8 weeks you should be ready to chop, and a huge yield of more than 600 grams per square yard of grow space isn't unusual!

Once they're harvested, you'll find it difficult to describe the stench of your Sour OG nugs. Though there are subtle hints of mint and that ever-present Skunk smell, the strongest aroma is a very Diesel-like, kerosene smell – the kind of smell that hits the air when you're hanging around with fire breathers. The high is just as exciting and will show you exactly why this is yet another great expression of the Diesel line.

Sour Pink Grapefruit

To quote good old Bill Shakespeare, "What's in a name?" Well, when it comes to this company, a lot. Holland's HortiLab really are horticultural scientists, and their grow rooms are more like labs than some labs I've been to, housing a large genetic library from which they make such fantastic strains as Sour Pink Grapefruit. Not many breeders have such breeding stock as the famed Sweet Pink Grapefruit to work with, but HortiLab do – and they've bred it with an East Coast Sour Diesel male to create a strain that definitely commands some attention.

You will need to keep a particularly close eye on these babies, though, as they grow so fast that they'll be reaching for the hot pans on the stove before you know it. You don't want to end up with burned plants, so be sure to raise your lights whenever necessary to keep the leaves from getting hurt. Odor control might become an issue for you in the later stages of flowering, as the Sour Diesel line is known to be stinkier than a vegetarian's fart after an eggplant curry, so good ventilation and charcoal filters will be your friends!

HortiLab Seed Company, Holland

Sativa-Dominant

Genetics: Sweet Pink Grapefruit x East Coast Sour Diesel V3

Potency: THC 14-20%

hortilab.nl

Your finished nugs will look good enough to eat, and when you finally smoke them, will set your heart pounding so far out of your chest you'll look like a Warner Bros. cartoon character who's just fallen in love.

Special K

Holland's Sagarmatha Seeds are single-handedly responsible for my diet turning to absolute shit in the last month or so. When I was gathering information for this book and decided to include their fantastic Special K strain, it sent me back down memory lane to when I spent a summer in England a few years ago. One day when I was browsing one of their horribly confusing supermarkets looking for a box of normal cereal to settle my craving for North Americans foods, I had a minor breakdown when I couldn't find any and bought this cereal called Special K Yoghurty instead. I think it's marketed for women trying to lose weight, but I got obsessed with it. All I did that summer was get high, eat copious amounts of Special K Yoghurty (the name is extra funny when you're baked) and walk around confused on their tiny sidewalks. Needless to say, researching this strain brought that all back so I ordered some online and have been eating nothing else for the last four weeks. Thanks, Sagarmatha.

I can't stay mad at them for long though; not when I've got a big fat bowl of this Western Winds x Slyder cross sat in front of my face just begging to be lit up. The Slyder parent is a cross between Northern Lights and an Afghani indica and brings a nice dose of indica genetics into a predominantly sativa plant. This makes Special K into a great indoor plant that grows with great internodal spacing and many bud sites. You'll see the Western Winds parentage come through in the bud growth, which gives long, thick, sparkling colas with hints of orange and green. These will grow fatter and fatter as your crop comes to the end of its 70-day flowering time, and will eventually give you a yield of around 350 grams of premium Special K bud per square yard of grow space. Trimming will be a walk in Hyde Park, as there are very few leaves packed around the buds, and the flowers look so beautiful anyway that you won't want to stop trimming them at all.

Sagarmatha Seeds, Holland

Sativa-Dominant

Genetics: Western Winds x Slyder

Potency: THC 18%

sagarmatha.nl

highestseeds.com

I can't help but feel that this strain is a lot more nutritious than the cereal it shares its name with. Not only does it taste sweet and feed your mind with a fast, strong effect, it lasts for ages, making it hours before you really need your next smoke. It should be noted that this is also a particularly great morning smoke, so now if you're British you can enjoy a bowl of Special K with your bowl of Special K Yoghurty – and your tea! I know you guys are obsessed with tea!

Speed Devil

Even the name of this strain gets my heart racing, as it makes me think of Taz, the Tasmanian Devil character who graced our TVs while we were growing up, and reminds me how I feel pretty much the same after smoking up some of these fantastic nugs. The name, however, is actually a reference to the plant's best two traits: its fantastically short flowering time and its truly wicked high.

Spain's Sweet Seeds have really outdone themselves here. Drawing on some fantastic Canadian auto-flowering genetics, they've created a plant that has a similar background to the popular Mighty Mite strain from the West coast. As with any ruderalis-influenced strain, Speed Devil flowers on its own schedule, regardless of lighting or season, so it requires a lot less trouble to grow than most other hybrids. The blossoming market for auto-flowering plants is a testament to the quality of ruderalis-inspired plants and how easy they are to grow. However, Speed Devil is even more perfect for the rookie grower than other auto-flowering strains as it is particularly resilient, so it'll survive a good number of stupid newbie mistakes before it goes sulking off into the world of the Could Have Been cannabis plants. It also won't grow beyond 2.5 feet, making it ideal for smaller grow spaces and even big closet grows. Using a fertilizer once a week while feeding is usually enough, as this girl is pretty self sufficient and doesn't need much help to reach her full potential and produce a ton of good bud.

Sweet Seeds, Spain

Sativa-Dominant

Genetics: Ruderalis x Indica/Sativa

Potency: THC 15%

sweetseeds.es

If, in the past, you've had problems controlling the humidity of your grow room, you'll be pleased to learn that Speed Devil has a great ability to fight off mold and other fungi, staying healthy even in less than perfect conditions. It has also been specially developed to be grown in the cramped, polluted environments of the inner cities that many of us find ourselves growing in. As much as we'd all love acres of outdoor grow space in the country, most of us don't have that, and Sweet Seeds knows this. Speed Devil really lives up to its name, as it will be ready for harvest just 5 weeks from planting – a phenomenal growth rate for such a fantastic plant.

Sweet Seeds seem to know their market very well; they know that many of us live in the city, and have not only created a strain that grows perfectly in this situation, they've created one that gives us the relaxing effect that people who deal with city life need, too! Speed Devil has a narcotic-like body effect as well as a spacey head high, leaving you stimulated and relaxed all at the same time.

Super Cali Haze

If I had to make a list of some of the breeders to watch in the current cannabis community, Stitch would certainly be up there. He's like the Sidney Crosby of the breeding world; he has far too much skill for someone his age and only seems to get better the older he gets. Thankfully Stitch doesn't complain quite as much as Crosby and doesn't take whole seasons out due to concussion. With this strain for Short Stuff Seedbank, Stitch has brought together two of the most classic sativa families of recent times; everyone's favorite high, Haze, and the infamous stinky Skunk. I can see you wriggling in your seat already; it's OK, I felt the same way when I first heard of this strain – but wait, there's more. Somewhere along the line Stitch has bred some ruderalis genetics into the mix, making this an auto-flowering sativa-dominant strain. Quick, someone, fetch a wet cloth; I'm about to faint!

Stitch's Nirvana Sky, an auto-flowering Haze plant, was created when a ruderalis plant was crossed with his special Haze plant and then backcrossed with a very resinous Colombian mother, forming the basis for Super Cali Haze. The most Haze-y phenotypes were crossed with a Skunk strain, helping to keep the flowering time down and preserve the much-loved traits of Haze. This strain can be grown both indoors and outdoors, it can reach up to 8 feet at its maximum height and it's at this height that it will reach its full potential. At this size, each plant can produce around 200 grams of gorgeous bud, and all without having to worry about vegetative times or forced flowering. Regardless of season, lighting, or teenage tantrums, Super Cali Haze will be ready for harvest at 120 days from seed, making this possibly the most simple sativa-dominant plant to grow in the history of growing. It is also perfect for growers who would like to harvest twice in one season – as well as lazy growers who love sativas but can't quite be bothered to grow 14-foot Lemon Haze plants!

Short Stuff Seedbank, breeder Stitch, Spain

Sativa-Dominant

Genetics: Haze x Skunk

Potency: THC 15%

shortstuffseeds.com

It almost feels bad to have a smoke this good for so little effort – as if I've cheated at a math test again or something. Thankfully, the effects of the smoke will quickly banish this feeling of guilt; in fact, they'll banish most other feelings that aren't pure ecstasy and loveliness. The high is pure sativa, straight from the 60s or 70s, but with 21st century cultivation technology. Imagine the feeling you'd get if they brought "Lost In Space" back, all with modern-day technology space shit…that's exactly how good you'll feel when you smoke up Super Cali Haze, except a bit more hungry.

Temple Haze

I've spoken before of my love of the Flying Dutchmen, and they continue to collect my admiration as they put out more and more great strains. In this instance, it would seem that I've got good taste, as they are very highly thought of in the wider cannabis community, too. Of course, everyone loves a good Haze strain, and with varieties such as this Temple Haze, it's inevitable that they would have quite the fan club. With Original Haze in the mix, you've got to be very careful which other plants you bring to the table; to pick the wrong strain would be like getting a prime piece of sirloin, cooking it for just a second until you get that amazing only-just-cooked feeling, savoring the delicious smell, then covering it with Thousand Island Dressing and potato chips. Thankfully the Flying Dutchmen are the haute cuisine chefs of the breeding game and found a strain more like a red wine reduction than a fatty, crap sauce; they bred Original Haze with a Nepali Hash Plant, and, my word, the resulting dish will have you salivating for more.

Flying Dutchmen, Holland

Sativa-Dominant

Genetics: Nepali x Original Haze

Potency: THC 17%

flyingdutchmen.com

With genetics that span the globe, from South American, Southeast Asian and the Himalayas, it's no surprise that this is a vivacious and wild-eyed plant that's difficult to keep down. As soon as these babies pop out of the soil they look like they're endlessly reaching for the sky above them with a dozen stringy arms, which eventually grow out into a large bushy tree and create a veritable Menorah of cannabis colas. These colas will continue to bloom and expand as the flowering stage goes on, so be sure to check regularly for mold or bud rot if your grow room has higher humidity levels; losing some of your stellar pot to one of these diseases is never a good thing. Temple Haze can be grown indoors or outdoors, although obviously due to its 6-foot size, any indoor crop will need to have a lot of space to fill out. You should expect to harvest at around 64 to 85 days, although use your own knowledge to figure out when your particular plants are ready. A microscope will help you with this!

As you would expect from any Hash Plant cross, Temple Haze colas will be covered with resin and will allow for great finger hash to be made after harvest; I'm sure you'll devour this in seconds, but be sure not to have too much. That distinctive Haze smell gives way to a high that is almost spiritual, being very dreamy and introspective inside your head while you're grinning like a madman on the outside.

Tha Purple Floss
(AKA Arianny Celeste)

Matt Riot of Riot Seeds may be the world's most well connected man. He seems to know every single person in the wider cannabis community, and thanks to this, his collection of genetics for breeding can actually be seen from space. For this strain, which is also known as Arianny Celeste after the stunning and apparently lovely UFC ring girl, the Riot Seeds breeders bred Chimera's Mental Floss with an Afgooey x Double Purple Doja from Bodhi Seeds, bringing together two of their favorite plants to create a strain that, like its namesake, is gorgeous and a total knockout!

This plant likes to play hard to get, and she'll make you wait a full 10 weeks before she lets you get at her buds. As the name might suggest, nugs from a Tha Purple Floss plant are fluffy and filled out, with a blue-purple tint that gives them endless bag appeal. These seeds are very, very limited edition, so be sure to grab some before they're gone; you won't be disappointed.

This toke is all sweetness and light, with a mild euphoria and excitability creeping over you when you're near it – again, much like its namesake. Sorry, Arianny – I'd choose this strain over you any day!

PHOTOS BY STAYHIGH

Riot Seeds, USA

Sativa-Dominant

Genetics: Mental Floss x (Afgooey x Double Purple Doja)

Potency: THC 19%

riotseeds.nl

The Void

This strain, from the famous Subcool and his Team Green Avengers crew, makes me think of days past when I was a newbie smoker and used to get myself so high I'd be unable to get off the couch or properly focus my eyes; a situation my friends and I used to call Entering The Void. Rather than just smoking mad amounts of Kush to create their Void, Subcool and TGA have bred together an Apollo-13 plant and a grape-tasting Querkle plant – which is a much more scientific way to do it.

A 60% sativa, The Void was first introduced in 2008. It grows well in a ScrOG set up, as well as in both hydro and soil set ups. It enjoys hot climates the most (don't we all?) and is especially at home in North America and Europe. The Void grows pretty tall but not obscenely so; it is still small enough to be grown indoors as well as out. An average yield is around 500 grams per 1000 watts of light, and the breeder recommends making bubble hash from The Void; it comes out pink!

This berry, slightly salty smoke results in a high that's clear, happy and social, meaning that you can smoke for a few hours at least without ending up with a body made of silly putty. If you smoke bowl after bowl for a few hours straight, however, there's definitely a chance that you, like me, might end up Entering The Void.

Subcool and Team Green Avengers, USA

Sativa-Dominant

Genetics: Apollo-13 x Querkle

Potency: THC 17-18%

tgagenetics.com

Thunderbud Haze

The UK's Holy Smoke Seeds is made up of some fantastic South African breeders who've relocated to Europe in order to make a splash on the huge cannabis scene there. They certainly have done that, with strains like the phenomenal indica-dominant Kong and this, a sativa-dominant variety known as Thunderbud Haze. To create this strain they used their own Thunderbud, a cross between their Pineapple Funk and a Clone Only Purple Urkel, and bred it with both a Strawberry Rez and SuperPurple Haze plant. The Thunderbud was first crossed two times with the Strawberry Rez, then they introduced their SuperPurple Haze into the mix. This veritable orgy of great genetics has given rise to a plant that's fruity, Hazey and a beauty all round.

This plant is a very easy one to grow, making it a good choice for newbie gardeners and especially those who've previously grown indica strains and are looking to move into the beautiful world of sativa cultivation. Through hard work and pure skill, Holy Smoke have managed to tame the wildest aspects of the sativas within Thunderbud Haze; the flowering time sits at around 8 weeks, and the plants grow to a medium height, getting slightly taller if you really want them to. The plants do tend to grow shorter and fatter than sativa growers will be used to, and they're able to be trained to grow in almost any grow space. Some growers will, in the vegetative stage, remove the lower branches to allow more growth to the top ones, and this can definitely work with a strain like Thunderbud Haze.

Holy Smoke Seeds, UK

Sativa-Dominant

Genetics: Thunderbud x Strawberry Rez x SuperPurple Haze

Potency: THC 19-21%

puresativa.com

When the flowering period begins, it will be as if your plants have suddenly developed an addiction to creamy coffees and doughnuts; they'll pack weight on as if from nowhere. The buds will swell almost before your eyes, blossoming into dense, slightly long nugs with several hints of color coming through. Expect a medium to high yield at the end of the flowering period, and treat your harvested nugs to a long curing period in order to bring out their phenomenal flavors.

Once you crack open your curing jars, your whole room will be overtaken by a smell of a dozen different fruits, from watermelon to strawberries with a little citrus twist, too. The Haze influence will be obvious thanks to the peppery scent, though if you miss that and forget it's there you'll be rudely reminded a few seconds later when the high hits you right between the eyes. Despite its pleasant odors, this is a very strong smoke and will be loved by veteran tokers rather than new kids on the block. Enjoy the strong body buzz with the active head high, but just don't have too much!

Tiger Stripe

America's BillBerry Farms are a very interesting company and one of the pioneers of tissue culture technology, which is being touted as the truest and best way to preserve quality genetics – even better than clones or seeds. Tiger Stripe is a Sonoma County strain created from New York Sour Diesel and Papaya from Nirvana Seeds, which began life as a tissue culture mutant. To me this means it could become a superhero at some point in the near future – but I could be wrong.

BillBerry Farms, USA,

Sativa-Dominant

Genetics: NY Sour

Diesel x Papaya

Potency: THC 19%

billberryfarmstissue-culture.com

Tiger Stripe plants prefer to be kept at around 6 feet, though they can grow up to 10 feet if you allow. They love to be sprayed in the vegetative stage, but do not like to be cloned at all. Be sure to keep these plants away from your lights, and spray lightly everyday. The breeder recommends a humidity level of 60% with the grow room at 75°F.

These conditions will give you near perfect Tiger Stripe buds; purple and orange nuggets with a sweet, fruity taste that will give you a very alert mindset with a calming body stone when you blaze them up. A great new strain to try!

Topa Mountain Purple Thai

Cali Gold Genetics, from the U.S., are a company known in North America for creating strains of the highest quality and using some very exceptional genetics. This reputation holds true for Topa Mountain Purple Thai, which was created from an Old School Fruity Thai and some Nigerian genetics dating back to the 70s.

When grown outside this strain becomes a specimen to behold; an extremely stretchy plant that just loves to create branches of 6 feet or more. It's a wild one, although its internodal spacing remains super tight, giving spears of sticky purple buds the size of Hulk Hogan's arm. For the absolute best growth, the breeder recommends employing topping, super cropping and the ScrOG technique in the vegetative stage. As you'd expect, this plant gives harvests of gigantic proportions; you'll be smoking Purple Thai buds for the next year and a half.

Cali Gold Genetics, USA

Sativa-Dominant

Genetics: Old School Heirloom Fruity Thai x 1970s Nigerian

Potency: THC 18.30%

caligoldgenetics.com

The buds of this strain have exotic notes of orange with purple candy and a woody note in there too. The high is textbook sativa; a soaring, glowing, social effect that feels like it's going on forever.

UK Pineapple

I'm not sure why, but I have a bit of a thing about stuff from the UK. Northern Soul, "Coronation Street," a pint at lunchtime, the idea of eating thick fries between two slices of bread; all these things just sit well with me. They make sense, ya know? The same goes for UK marijuana strains; I had a six-month period when all I would smoke was UK Cheese, and I'm just about to get into the same situation with this UK Pineapple. Sonic Seeds have done a great job in combining some fantastically unusual genetics to create a strain that is not only a killer smoke but also carries the spirit of Britain's joyous multiculturalism; it's a cross between an 80s Skunk and a strain from Jamaica!

First created fourteen years ago, UK Pineapple began life as a 1982 SK1 from a clone which was thankfully well preserved. Around the same time, a friend of the breeder came back from a trip to Jamaica with an amazing Skunk hybrid being grown in Westmoreland, which Sonic Seeds then crossed with a plant from a small field of Alaskan that they also had. The resultant hybrid was then crossed with the SK1 plant to create the strain that we have today. UK Pineapple also makes great breeding stock, as almost anything crossed with it then becomes a huge, huge yielder!

Sonic Seeds, UK

Sativa-Dominant

Genetics: 1982 SK1 x Westmoreland Jamaican Alaska

Potency: THC 20%

cannaseur.com

breedbay.co.uk

This is a strain that could be cultivated in a whole range of situations. I know of UK Pineapple being grown in 10 x 10-foot grow tents, medium grow rooms and even outside, too, as they can be kept to knee height or allowed to grow tall. They are perfectly happy being grown in a flood and drain system as well as an organic soil grow. You can harvest these plants at around 9 weeks, but if you can wait, pushing the harvest date back until 12 weeks will give you so much sick bud that you'll have to have a month-long smoking party to get rid of it all. Towards the end of the flowering stage UK Pineapple's aroma can be very hard to control, with a very noticeable Skunk edge and a sweet fruit smell, too. Be sure to ventilate well and use carbon filters.

You'll get some mad red eye from your first bowl of UK Pineapple, as well as a stone that hits you like one of the rocks from Stonehenge falling on your body. The taste of banana and peaches will dance on your tongue right before turning you into the World's most Stereotypical Stoner: sore eyes, dry mouth, inability to say much beyond "man...." It's awesome!

Uncle Lucious's Lemonade

SKUNK Magazine's Cultivation Editor, the Rev, has quite the following these days. His True Living Organics grow style has converted many from chemical-based grow ops to a more natural environment. His seeds, too, are grown 100% organic, and an extensive breeding stock means that he always comes up with new and interesting varieties to please his many fans. Uncle Lucious's Lemonade is a blend of Arcata Lemonwreck, Metal Haze and Cindy 99 genetics. She is a 75% sativa strain that first appeared in 2006 and has been lighting up grow rooms ever since.

An "anywhere" strain, she grows best indoors in an environment with lower humidity. It can take well to a ScrOG set up, although SOG would be a better choice and, of course, this should only ever be grown organically in soil. Check out the Rev's own True Living Organics grow style for optimum results!

60 days after forced flowering you should end up with about 30 grams of primo pot per gallon of soil mix used. With great pain-killing effects and a taste that's addictive, Uncle Lucious's Lemonade is a fantastic strain.

PHOTOS BY THE REV

Kingdom Organic Seeds by The Rev, USA

Sativa-Dominant

Genetics: Arcata Lemonwreck x Metal Haze/C99

facebook.com/
KingdomOrganicSeeds
facebook.com/
TrueLivingOrganics

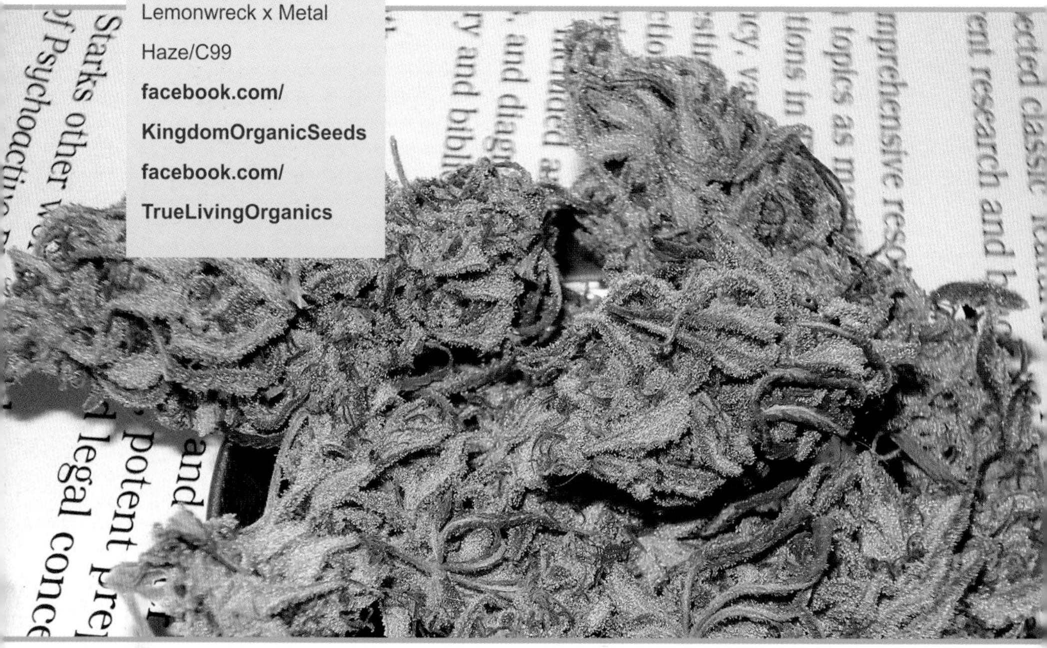

Verhdaj

Go on; pronounce that name. I dare you. No? Neither can I, and that's because Verhdaj is the first Slovenian strain I've had the pleasure of featuring in these strain guides – and I think this might be the first Slovenian strain in ANY strain guide! Our Slovenian grower friend, Andrej, created this variety from an old sativa/indica seed mix which he's been working with for so long he no longer knows the origin of it – now that is hardcore breeding!

Andrej has been breeding Verhdaj (which sounds like a sneeze when I try to say it) for many years now, and named the strain, also called Verhdajka, after the old farm on which it was grown. It is a very simple strain to cultivate, and has only been bred outdoors before. It doesn't need any specific nutrients and growing techniques, and will take well almost anywhere. As a heavy sativa-dominant, it grows taller than 6 feet and will yield over 2 pounds by the time harvest rolls around at the end of September! Anyone else thinking about moving to Slovenia with me now?

Secret Slovenian Grower

Andrej, Slovenia

Sativa-Dominant

Genetics: Unknown

Potency: THC 17%

The finished orange and green Verhdaj buds will smell fruity with an acidic hint, and when you light up your first bowl you'll taste sweet vanilla and orange peel. The effect is just as sweet: a flying high that seems to never let go. Amazing.

Cannabis Sativa The Essential Guide to the World's Finest Marijuana Strains, Volume 2

Whippet

America's Stoney Girl Gardens are something of a phenomenon; a collective of legal growers who provide classes on how to grow your own medicine as well as 100% organic seeds and some strains that will blow your mind. They specialize in very heavy hitting, almost narcotic strains for relief of extreme pain, and Whippet definitely falls into this category. A cross between Stoney Girl's own Berkeley and Pit Bill, the latter of which is a blend of Sugar Plum with their insanely hard-hitting P-91, Whippet is a sativa-dominant strain with enough kick to push you right into another dimension!

As an ongoing project, this strain is bound to get better and better with time, but it's definitely no slouch as it is right now. With a maximum height of 3-5 feet, it can be grown both indoors and out, although it favors temperatures of around 70 Fahrenheit in its grow area. It's fairly resistant to both pests and mold, and is easy to grow for beginners as well as experienced cultivators. Expect a yield of 120 grams after a relatively short flowering period of just 30 days.

Stoney Girl Gardens, USA

Sativa-Dominant

Genetics: Berkeley x Pit Bull

Potency: THC 28%

gro4me.com

stoneygirlgardens.com

Though these buds don't have much flavor, the Whippet high is just like the dog it's named after: very rushy, focused and extremely playful. It's also great for killing chronic pain in medical patients and for everyone else, it's just a fantastic toke.

White Jack

Though this strain sounds like a professional listing of the White Stripes' frontman, it's actually got a lot more in common with Bob Marley than it has with Jack. Produced by the UK's reggae-loving seed company Dready Seeds, White Jack makes no surprises by being a cross between White Widow and a Jack Herer plant, two strains that every toker worth their kief has heard of, possibly grown and definitely loved at some point in their lives.

Coming in at 12 feet with a seriously expansive structure, White Jack might well be the first marijuana plant to be seen from space. Unlike its namesake, who always seems more happy in the shade, White Jack needs a hell of a lot of sunlight and lots of water to keep it hydrated. It's resistant to mold and even when planted later in the season won't succumb to bud rot, no matter how humid it gets. The flowering period sits at around 70 days, meaning that you should get everyone you know round to help with harvest on October 25th. You'll most definitely need their help in cutting down your mammoth yield, and they'll be more than happy to oblige!

Dready Seeds, UK

Sativa-Dominant

Genetics: Jack Herer x White Widow

Potency: THC 16-20%

dreadyseeds.com

Growing this strain organically, as intended, will help accentuate its phenomenal pepper and citrus smell which will set you up for the heavy sedative high as it sings you to sleep with a lullaby or two.

White Stone

Spain's Evil Seeds might sound intimidating, but deep down they're as sweet as puppy dogs; if they were in any way diabolical they would never have given the world such a brilliant hybrid as White Stone – which, incidentally, sounds like a gathering place for druids at the UK's Stonehenge, so it's certainly not evil. A cross between the much-loved White Widow and a Rosetta Stone plant from the Brothers Grimm, White Stone is a slightly sativa-dominant variety that's a great choice for medical users the world over!

Our Spanish breeder friends have put a lot of effort into creating a robust and sturdy plant that's easy to grow, so that medical patients taking their first foray into growing can have some powerful medicine without breaking too much of a sweat. The thick stems and bushy, indica-like growth patterns of White Stone make it simple to look after, and mean that it shouldn't need any help in carrying its own large buds towards the end of flowering.

When harvested, your buds will be very dense and compact with a floral bouquet that smells like the first flush of spring. Medical patients will absolutely love this strain for its high power and its pain-killing abilities. Just one toke will leave you convinced that Evil Seeds are nothing short of angelic.

Evil Seeds, Spain

Sativa-Dominant

Genetics: White Widow x Rosetta Stone

Potency: THC 20-22%

evilseeds.es

PHOTOS BY CRAIG

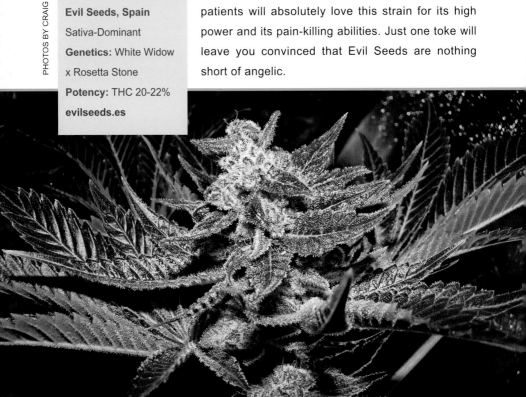

Wombat

Spain's Blim Burn Seeds may be fairly new, compared to many seed companies, but they are already carving themselves out a sturdy reputation in the European scene and abroad. I would like to think that this has a lot to do with their incredibly awesome logos – each strain has its own distinct one, and the Wombat one might be the cutest thing I've ever seen – but in my heart of hearts I know that it's because they make incredibly psychoactive strains that take you into the stratosphere. Wombat is a great example of this, as the Critical Mass and Haze parent strains have combined to create a strain that can turn your garden fence blue and leave you wondering where exactly you put your feet.

Wombat, unlike its marsupial namesake, is a speedy devil, and its hybrid vigor and strong growth mean that you can skip the vegetative stage entirely and flip your plant into flowering directly. In fact, it must be this sturdy structure that gives this strain its name; although they look cute, wombats are in fact solid critters than can smash into a fully grown man and bowl him over badly enough to break some bones! Wombat plants are much the same; they don't look like the most intimidating things in the world, reaching a height of around 3 feet on average, but they're pretty hardcore and difficult to break! Despite the majority sativa influence the indica structure wins through giving wombat-shaped trees; thick and fairly short with a mean girth. This strain can be grown indoors, but it is easiest to grow outdoors where it will pretty much take care of itself, and where its branch strength protects it from breakages in high winds. As well as a tight, dense structure, the indica influence of this strain brings its flowering time down to around 63 days – much shorter than some of the majority sativa plants. If you are lucky enough to grow this strain outdoors, you should be looking to harvest around October 15th in the Northern hemisphere, or around mid-April if you are from the land down under. With good conditions and a bit of care, you can expect the plants to yield around 650 grams per square yard of grow space.

Blim Burn Seeds, Spain

Sativa-Dominant

Genetics: Moby Dick x Critical Mass

Potency: THC 18%

blimburnseeds.com

semillasdemarihuana.net

Wombat produces buds that are very large and very dense, yet quite subtle in their aroma; give the nugs a good sniff and you'll see what I mean. Their taste is somewhat less subdued, with a great sweetness from the indica parent giving way to a Haze flavor that's more welcome than an umbrella salesman in a storm! The high will set your mind on fire – just don't overdo it and end up thinking you're a marsupial yourself.

Wreckage

Holland's TH Seeds absolutely love their own S.A.G.E. strain – and I'm not talking regular love here. I'm talking the sort of love that leads a father to sit his daughter's date down before the prom and threaten to break his legs if he does anything more than kiss her on the cheek; that kind of love. The TH Seeds breeders have been so protective of S.A.G.E. – or Sativa Afghani Genetic Equilibrium – since it was born that it has pretty much been living in one of those protective bubbles and has only been allowed to meet the most genetically inspiring peer plants, even for a friendly cup of tea. The fact that the breeders have allowed baby S.A.G.E. to hook up with Trainwreck, then, says a lot about how much respect they have for the Clone Only strain – and how much they expect from this little offspring!

Both of Wreckage's parent plants have flying sativa highs and phenomenal tastes, but they differ greatly in some ways – as every good couple do. In this case, it's the way they grow that sets them apart; while Trainwreck is a wild-eyed, crazy grower, S.A.G.E. is a more mature and down-to-earth plant who keeps her partner's excessive traits under control. Though Wreckage plants will grow extremely quickly at first, they respond excellently to topping after which they tend to make equal tops and sit at around the same height as their friends. They also tend to show their sex faster than some sativa-dominant plants, meaning that you can separate out your males before they do any damage. You'll see very healthy deep green leaves on your plants, which should reach about 5 feet in total, but remember to give them lots and lots of light to keep them super happy and perky. The Trainwreck parent plant can be difficult to deal with, so any finicky traits that have passed over into Wreckage can be attributed to its poppa plant. Keep a good eye on your crop for signs of under- or overwatering and all should be good. Wreckage's flowering time is 65 days, and you should expect to yield 350 grams of bud per square yard of grow space.

TH Seeds, Holland

Sativa-Dominant

Genetics: S.A.G.E. x Trainwreck

Potency: 19%

thseeds.com

The first thing that you'll notice about your Wreckage high is that your tongue is completely numb. Don't worry though, you won't be having a medical emergency any time soon; just a taste attack as the flavors of pine and mint converge in your mouth and start having a little party. The sativa high that results from this strain comes from both of the parent strains, and as such packs a hella powerful head high along with a tingly body buzz that stops you from forgetting that your body is there. A beauty of a strain – but don't believe me, get some for yourself!

X-Dog

Spain's Alpine Seeds are really becoming big players in the scene these days. With such solid and dependable strains as Erdbeer and Sweet Chunk under their belt, they've established themselves as consistently good breeders and X-Dog is another example of their skill. A three-way cross between the classic Northern Lights, White Widow and the elusive ChemDawg, this is a 60% sativa dominant strain with a very strong buzz.

X-Dog expresses herself in two phenotypes, one closer to the ChemDawg father and the other much more like the NLX mother. Both of these expressions grow best indoors, where they will reach a medium height and not get so leggy that your grow space becomes a giant spider's web of branches. They will love soil systems but don't do well in ScrOG set ups, so avoid that one! The average flowering time for either phenotype is 65 days, and when harvest comes around you can claim about 35 grams from a plant that's between 3 and 4 feet — not too shabby for a plant that's so easy to grow! The buds will be particularly resinous, too, thanks to the influence of the shimmering Chem-Dawg father plant. They're a sight to behold!

Alpine Seeds, Spain

Sativa-Dominant

Genetics: (Northern Lights x White Widow) x ChemDawg (dd)

Potency: THC 18%

alpine-seeds.net

You'll want to wear your orange- and ice-frosted nugs as bling, but if you can bring yourself to smoke them you'll be rewarded with a perfect party high: social, energetic and all up in the head. What more could you ask for?

Index

Index

Index

Index

The World's Most Comprehensive and Detailed Strain Guides

Each Book Features 100 Amazing Strains from 100 Amazing Breeders!

No other strain guide series has featured this many breeders and strains before!